The Two Covenants

and

The Second Blessing

Andrew Murray

Bibliographic Information

The Two Covenants was previously published in London by JAMES NISBET & CO. LTD., 21 BERNERS STREET, W. This classic reprint reflects the text of the 1899 edition.

an Ichthus Publications edition

ISBN 10: 1502883007
ISBN 13: 978-1502883001

www.ichthuspublications.com

CONTENTS

3

INTRODUCTION

I T IS OFTEN SAID that the great aim of the preacher ought to be to translate Scripture truth from its Jewish form into the language and the thought of the nineteenth century, and so to make it intelligible and acceptable to our ordinary Christians. It is to be feared that the experiment will do more harm than good. In the course of the translation the force of the original is lost. The scholar who trusts to translations will never become a master of the language he wants to learn. A race of Christians will be raised up, to whom the language of God's Word, and with that the God who spoke it, will be strange. In the Scripture words not a little of Scripture truth will be lost. For the true Christian life nothing is so healthful and invigorating as to have each man come and study for himself the very words in which the Holy Ghost has spoken.

One of the words of Scripture, which is almost going out of fashion, is the word Covenant. There was a time when it was the keynote of the theology and the Christian life of strong and holy men. We know how deep in Scotland it entered into the national life and thought. It made mighty men, to whom God, and His promise and power were wonderfully real. It will be found still to bring strength and purpose to those who will take the trouble to bring all their life under control of the inspiring assurance that they are living in covenant with a God who has sworn faithfully to fulfil in them every promise He has given.

This book is a humble attempt to show what exactly the blessings are that God has covenanted to bestow on us; what the assurance is the Covenant gives that they must, and can, and will be fulfilled; what the hold on God Himself is which it thus gives us; and what the conditions are for the full and continual experience of its blessings. I feel confident that if I can lead any to listen to what God has to say to them of His Covenant, and to deal with Him as a Covenant God, it will bring them strength and joy.

Not long ago I received from one of my correspondents a letter with the following passage in it:—

> "I think you will excuse and understand me when I say there is one further note of power I would like so much to have introduced into your next book on Intercession. God Himself has, I know, been giving me some direct teaching this winter upon the place the New Covenant is to have in intercessory prayer . . . I know you believe in the Covenant, and the Covenant rights we have on account of it. Have you followed out your views of the Covenant as they bear upon this subject of intercession? Am I wrong in coming to the conclusion that we may come boldly into God's presence, and not only ask, but claim a Covenant right through Christ Jesus to all the spiritual searching, and cleansing, and knowledge, and power promised in the three great Covenant promises? If you would take the Covenant and speak of it as God could enable you to speak, I think that would be the quickest way the Lord could take to make His Church wake up to the power He has put into our hands in giving us a Covenant. I would be so glad if you would tell God's people that *they have a Covenant.*"

Though this letter was not the occasion of the writing of the book, and our Covenant rights have been considered in a far wider aspect than their relation to prayer, I am persuaded that nothing will help us more in our work of intercession, than the entrance for ourselves personally into what it means that we have a Covenant God.

My one great desire has been to ask Christians whether they are really seeking to find out what exactly God wants them to be, and is willing to make them. It is only as they want, "that the mind of the Lord may be showed them," that their faith can ever truly see, or accept, or enjoy what God calls "His salvation." As long as we expect God to do for us what we ask or think, we limit Him. When we believe that as high as the heavens are above the earth, His thoughts are above our thoughts, and wait on Him as God to do unto us *according to His word,* as He means, we shall be prepared to live the truly supernatural, heavenly life the Holy Spirit can work in us—the true Christ life.

May God lead every reader into the secret of His presence, and "show him His Covenant."

ANDREW MURRAY, *Wellington, South Africa*

The Two Covenants

1
The Two Covenants

"Know therefore that the Lord thy God, He is God, the faithful God, which keepeth covenant and mercy with them that love Him and keep His commandments" (Deuteronomy 7:9).

MEN OFTEN MAKE COVENANTS. They know the advantages to be derived from them. As an end of enmity or uncertainty, as a statement of services and benefits to be rendered, as a security for their certain performance, as a bond of amity and goodwill, as a ground for perfect confidence and friendship, a covenant has often been of unspeakable value.

In His infinite condescension to our human weakness and need, there is no possible way in which men pledge their faithfulness, that God has not sought to make use of, to give us perfect confidence in Him, and the full assurance of all that He, in His infinite riches and power as God, has promised to do to us. It is with this view He has consented to bind Himself by covenant, as if He could not be trusted. Blessed is the man who truly knows God as his Covenant God; who knows what the Covenant promises him; what unwavering confidence of expectation it secures, that all its terms will be fulfilled to him; what a claim and hold it gives him on the Covenant-keeping God Himself. To many a man, who has never thought much of the Covenant, a true and living faith in it would mean the transformation of his whole life. *The full knowledge of what God wants to do* for him; *the assurance that it will be done* by an Almighty Power; *the being drawn to God Himself* in personal surrender, and dependence, and waiting to have it done; all this would make the Covenant the very gate of heaven. May the Holy Spirit give us some vision of its glory.

When God created man in His image and likeness, it was that he might have a life as like His own as it was possible for a creature to live. This was to be by God Himself living and working all in man. For this man was to yield himself in loving dependence to the wonderful glory of being the recipient, the bearer, the manifestation of a Divine life. The one secret of man's happiness was to be a trustful surrender of his whole being to the willing and the working of God. When sin entered, this relation to God was destroyed; when man had disobeyed, he feared God and fled from Him. He no longer knew, or loved, or trusted God.

Man could not save himself from the power of sin. If his redemption was to be effected, God must do it all. And if God was to do it in harmony with the law of man's nature, man must be brought to desire it, to yield his willing consent, and entrust himself to God. All that God wanted man to do was, to believe in Him. What a man believes, moves and rules his whole being, enters into him, and becomes part of his very life. Salvation could only be by faith: God restoring the life man had lost; man in faith yielding himself to God's work and will. The first great work of God with man was to get him to believe. This work cost God more care and time and patience than we can easily conceive. All the dealings with individual men, and with the people of Israel, had just this one object, to teach men to trust Him. Where He found faith He could do anything. Nothing dishonoured and grieved Him so much as unbelief. Unbelief was the root of disobedience and every sin; it made it impossible for God to do His work. The one thing God sought to waken in men by promise and threatening, by mercy and judgment, was faith.

Of the many devices of which God's patient and condescending grace made use to stir up and strengthen faith, one of the chief was— the Covenant. In more than one way God sought to effect this by His Covenant. First of all, His Covenant was always *a revelation of His purposes,* holding out, in definite promise, what God was willing to work in those with whom the Covenant was made. It was a Divine pattern of the work God intended to do in their behalf, that they might know what to desire and expect, that their faith might nourish itself with the very things, though as yet unseen, which God was working out. Then, the Covenant was meant to be a *security and guarantee,* as simple and plain and humanlike as the Divine glory could make it, that the very things which

God had promised would indeed be brought to pass and wrought out in those with whom He had entered into covenant Amid all delay and disappointment and apparent failure of the Divine promises, the Covenant was to be the anchor of the soul, pledging the Divine veracity and faithfulness and unchangeableness for the certain performance of what had been promised. And so the Covenant was, above all, to give man *a hold upon God,* as the Covenant-keeping God, to link him to God Himself in expectation and hope, to bring him to make God Himself alone the portion and the strength of his soul.

Oh that we knew how God longs that we should trust Him, and how surely His every promise must be fulfilled to those who do so! Oh that we knew how it is owing to nothing but our unbelief that we cannot enter into the possession of God's promises, and that God cannot— yes, cannot—do His mighty works in us, and for us, and through us! Oh that we knew how one of the surest remedies for our unbelief—the divinely chosen cure for it—is the Covenant into which God has entered with us! The whole dispensation of the Spirit, the whole economy of grace in Christ Jesus, the whole of our spiritual life, the whole of the health and growth and strength of the Church, has been laid down and provided for, and secured in the New Covenant. No wonder that, where that Covenant, with its wonderful promises, is so little thought of, its plea for an abounding and unhesitating confidence in God so little understood, its claim upon the faithfulness of the Omnipotent God so little tested; no wonder that Christian life should miss the joy and the strength, the holiness and the heavenliness which God meant and so clearly promised that it should have.

Let us listen to the words in which God's Word calls us to know, and worship, and trust our Covenant-keeping God—it may be we shall find what we have been looking for: the deeper, the full experience of all God's grace can do in us. In our text Moses says: *"Know therefore* that the Lord thy God, He is God, *the faithful God, which keepeth covenant* with them that love Him." Hear what God says in Isaiah: "The mountains shall depart, and the hills be removed; but My kindness shall not depart from thee, *neither shall My covenant of peace be removed,* saith the Lord that hath mercy on thee." More sure than any mountain is the fulfilment of every Covenant promise. Of the New Covenant, in Jeremiah, God speaks: *"I will make an everlasting covenant with them, that I will not turn away from them,* to do them good; but I will put My fear in their hearts, that they shall not depart from Me." The Covenant secures alike that God will not turn from us, nor we depart from Him: He undertakes both for Himself and us.

Let us ask very earnestly whether the lack in our Christian life, and specially in our faith, is not owing to the neglect of the Covenant. We have not worshipped nor trusted the Covenant-keeping God. Our soul has not done what God called us to—"to take hold of His Covenant," "to remember the Covenant"; is it wonder that our faith has failed and come short of the blessing? God could not fulfil His promises in us. If we will begin to examine into the terms of the Covenant, as the title-deeds of our inheritance, and the riches we are to possess even here on earth; if we will think of the certainty of their fulfilment, more sure than the foundations of the everlasting mountains; if we will turn to the God who has engaged to do all for us, who keepeth covenant for ever, our life will become different from what it has been; it can, and will be, all that God would make it.

The great lack of our religion is—we need more of God. We accept salvation as His gift, and we do not know that the only object of salvation, its chief blessing, is to fit us for, and bring us back to, *that close intercourse with God* for which we were created, and in which our glory in eternity will be found. All that God has ever done for His people in making a covenant was always to bring them to Himself as their chief, their only good, to teach them to trust in Him, to delight in Him, to be one with Him. It cannot be otherwise. If God, indeed, be nothing but a very fountain of goodness and glory, of beauty and blessedness, the more we can have of His presence, the more we conform to His will, the more we are engaged in His service, the more we have Him ruling and working all in us, the more truly happy shall we be. And that only is a true and good religious life, which brings us every day nearer to this God, which makes us give up everything to have more of Him. No obedience can be too strict, no dependence too absolute, no submission too complete, no confidence too implicit, to a soul that is learning to count God Himself its chief good, its exceeding joy.

In entering into covenant with us, God's one object, is to draw us to Himself, to render us entirely dependent upon Himself, and so to bring us into the right position and disposition in which He can fill us with Himself, His love, and His blessedness. Let us undertake our study of the New Covenant, in which, if we are believers, God is at this moment living and walking with us, with the honest purpose and surrender, at any price, to know what God wishes to be to us, to do in us, and to have us be and do to Him. The New Covenant may become to us one of the windows of heaven through which we see into the face, into the very heart, of God.

2
The Two Covenants: Their Relation

"It is written, that Abraham had two sons, one by the bondmaid, and one by the freewoman. Howbeit, the one by the bondmaid is born after the flesh; but the son by the freewoman is born through promise. Which things contain an allegory: for these women are two covenants" (Galatians 4:22-24).

THERE ARE TWO COVENANTS, one called the Old, the other the New. God speaks of this very distinctly in Jeremiah, where He says: "The days come, that I will make a new covenant with the house of Israel, not after the covenant I made with their fathers" (Jer. 31). This is quoted in Hebrews, with the addition: "In that He saith a new covenant, He hath made the first old." Our Lord spoke Himself of the New Covenant in His blood. In His dealings with His people, in His working out His great redemption, it has pleased God that there should be two covenants.

It has pleased Him, not as an arbitrary appointment, but for good and wise reasons, which made it indispensably necessary that it should be so, and no otherwise. The clearer our insight into the reasons, and the Divine reasonableness, of there thus being two covenants, and into their relation to each other, the more full and true can be our own personal apprehension of what the New Covenant is meant to be to us. They indicate two stages in God's dealing with man; two ways of serving God, a lower or elementary one of preparation and promise, a higher or more advanced one of fulfilment and possession. As that in which the true excellency of the second consists is opened up to us, we can spiritually enter into what God has prepared for us. Let us try and understand why there should have been two, neither less nor more.

The reason is to be found in the fact that, in religion, in all intercourse between God and man, there are two parties, and that each of them must have the opportunity to prove what their part is in the Covenant. In the Old Covenant man had the opportunity given him to prove what He could do, with the aid of all the means of grace God could bestow. That Covenant ended in man proving his own unfaithfulness and failure. In the New Covenant, God is to prove what He can do with man, all unfaithful and feeble as he is, when He is allowed and trusted *to do all the work.* The Old Covenant was one dependent on man's obedience, one which he could break, and did break (Jer. 31:32). The New Covenant was one which God has engaged shall never be broken; *He Himself keeps it and ensures our keeping it: so He makes it an Everlasting Covenant.*

It will repay us richly to look a little deeper into this. This relation of God to fallen man in covenant is the same as it was to unfallen man as Creator. And what was that relation? God proposed to make a man in His own image and likeness. The chief glory of God is that He has life in Himself; that He is independent of all else, and owes what He is to Himself alone. If the image and likeness of God was not to be a mere name, and man was really to be like God in the power to make himself what he was to be, he must needs have the power of free will and self-determination. This was the problem God had to solve in man's creation in His image. Man was to be a creature made by God, and yet he was to be, as far as a creature could be, like God, self-made. In all God's treatment of man these two factors were ever to be taken into account. God was ever to take the initiative, and be to man the source of life. Man was ever to be the recipient, and yet at the same time the disposer of the life God bestowed.

When man had fallen through sin, and God entered into a covenant of salvation, these two sides of the relationship had still to be maintained intact. God was ever to be the first, and man the second. And yet man, as made in God's image, was ever, as second, to have full time and opportunity to appropriate or reject what God gave, to prove how far he could help himself, and indeed be self-made. His absolute dependence upon God was not to be forced upon him; if it was really to be a thing of moral worth and true blessedness, it must be his deliberate and voluntary choice. And this now is the reason why there was a first and a second covenant, that in the first, man's desires and efforts might be fully awakened, and time given for him to make full proof of what his human nature, with the aid of outward instruction and miracles and means of grace, could accomplish. When his utter impotence, his hopeless captivity under the power of sin had been discovered, there came the New Covenant, in which God was to reveal how man's true liberty from sin and self and the creature, his true nobility and God-likeness, was to be found in the most entire and absolute dependence, *in God's being and doing all within him.*

In the very nature of things there was no other way possible to God than this in dealing with a being whom He had endowed with the Godlike power of a will. And all the weight this reason for the Divine procedure has in God's dealing with His people as a whole, it equally has in dealing with the individual. The two covenants represent two stages of God's education of man and of man's seeking after God. The progress and transition from the one to the other is not merely chronological or historical; it is organic and spiritual. In greater or lesser degree it is seen in every member of the body, as well as in the body as a whole. Under the Old Covenant there were men in whom, by anticipation, the powers of the coming redemption worked mightily. In the New Covenant there are men in whom the spirit of the Old still makes itself manifest. The New Testament proves, in some of its most important epistles,—especially those to the Galatians, Romans, and Hebrews,—how possible it is within the New Covenant still to be held fast in the bondage of the Old.

This is the teaching of the passage from which our text is taken. In the home of Abraham, the father of the faithful, Ishmael and Isaac are both found—the one born of a slave, the other of a free woman; the one after the flesh and the will of man, the other through the promise and the power of God; the one only for a time, then to be cast out, the other to be heir of all. A picture held up to the Galatians of the life they were leading, as they trusted to the flesh and its religion, making a fair show, and yet proved, by their being led captive to sin, to be, not of the free but of the bond woman. Only through faith in the promise and the mighty quickening power of God could they, could any of them, be made truly and fully free, and stand in the freedom with which Christ has made us free.

As we proceed to study the two covenants in the light of this and other scriptures, we shall see how they are indeed the Divine revelation of two systems of religious worship, each with its spirit or life-principle ruling every man who professes to be a Christian. We shall see how the one great cause of the feebleness of so many Christians is just this, that the Old Covenant spirit of bondage still has the mastery. And we shall see that nothing but a spiritual insight, with a whole-hearted acceptance, and a living experience, of all the New Covenant engages *that God will work in us,* can possibly fit for walking as God would have us do.

This truth of there being two stages in our service of God, two degrees of nearness in our worship, is typified in many things in the Old Covenant worship; perhaps nowhere more clearly than in the difference between the Holy Place and the Most Holy Place in the temple, with the veil separating them. Into the former the priests might always enter to draw near to God. And yet they might not come too near; the veil kept them at a distance. To enter within that, was death. Once a year the High Priest might enter, as a promise of the time when the veil should be taken away and the full access to dwell in God's presence be given to His people. In Christ's death the veil of the temple was rent, and His blood gives us boldness and power to enter into the Holiest of all and live there day by day in the immediate presence of God. It is by the Holy Spirit, who issued forth from that Holiest of all, where Christ had entered, to bring its life to us, and make us one with it, that we can have the power to live and walk always with the consciousness of God's presence in us.

It is thus not only in Abraham's home that there were the types of the two covenants, the spirit of bondage and the spirit of liberty, but even in God's home in the temple. The priests had not yet the liberty of access into the Father's presence. Not only among the Galatians, but everywhere throughout the Church, there are to be found two classes of Christians. Some are content with the mingled life, half flesh and half spirit, half self-effort and half grace. Others are not content with this, but are seeking with their whole heart to know to the full what the deliverance from sin and what the abiding full power for a walk in God's presence is, which the New Covenant has brought and can give. God help us all to be satisfied with nothing less.[1]

---

[1] See Note A, on the Second Blessing.

3
The First Covenant

"Now therefore, if ye will obey My voice, and keep My covenant, ye shall be a peculiar treasure unto Me" (Exodus 19:5).

"He declared unto you His covenant, which He commanded you to perform, even ten commandments" (Deuteronomy 4:13).

"If ye keep these judgments, the Lord thy God shall keep unto thee the covenant" (Deuteronomy 7:12).

"I will make a new covenant with the house of Israel, not according to the covenant which I made with their fathers, which My covenant they brake" (Jeremiah 31:31-32).

WE HAVE SEEN HOW the reason for there being two Covenants is to be found in the need of giving the Divine and the human will, each their due place in the working out of man's destiny. God ever takes the initiative. Man must then have the opportunity to do his part, and to prove either what he can do, or needs to have done for him. The Old Covenant was on the one hand indispensably necessary to waken man's desires, to call forth his efforts, to deepen the sense of dependence on God, to convince of his sin and impotence, and so to prepare him to feel the need of the salvation of Christ. In the significant language of Paul, "The law was our schoolmaster unto Christ." "We were kept under the law, shut up unto the faith, which should afterwards be revealed." To understand the Old Covenant aright we must ever remember its two great characteristics— the one, that it was of Divine appointment, fraught with much true blessing, and *absolutely indispensable* for the working out of God's purposes; the other, that it was only provisional and preparatory to something higher, and therefore *absolutely insufficient* for giving that full salvation which man needs if his heart or the heart of God is to be satisfied.

Note now the terms of this first Covenant. *"If ye* will obey My voice and keep My covenant, ye shall be unto Me a holy nation." Or, as it is expressed in Jeremiah (7:23; 11:4), "Obey My voice, and I will be your God." Obedience everywhere, especially in the Book of Deuteronomy, appears as the condition of blessing. "A blessing, if ye obey" (11:27). Some may ask how God could make a covenant of which He knew that man could not keep it. The answer opens up to us the whole nature and object of the Covenant. All education, Divine or human, ever deals with its pupils on the principle—faithfulness in the less is essential to the attainment of the greater. In taking Israel into His training, God dealt with them as men in whom, with all the ruin sin had brought, there still was a conscience to judge of good and evil, a heart capable of being stirred to long after God, and a will to choose the good and to choose Himself. Before Christ and His salvation could be revealed and understood and truly appreciated, these faculties of man had to be stirred and wakened. The law took men into its training, and sought, if I may use the expression, to make the very best that could be made of them by external instruction. In the provision made in the law for a symbolical atonement and pardon, in all God's revelation of Himself through priest and prophet and king, in His interposition in providence and grace, everything was done that He could do, to touch and win the heart of His people and to give force to the appeal to their self-interest or their gratitude, their fear or their love.

Its work was not without fruit. Under the law, administered by the grace that ever accompanied it, there was trained up a number of men whose great mark was the fear of God, and a desire to walk blameless in all His commandments. And yet, as a whole, Scripture represents the Old Covenant as a failure. The law had promised life; but it could not give it (Deut. 4:1; Gal. 3:21). The real purpose for which God had given it was the very opposite: it was meant by Him as "a ministration of death." He gave it that it might convince man of his sin, and might so waken the confession of his impotence, and of his need of a New

Covenant and a true redemption. It is in this view that Scripture uses such strong expressions—"By the law is *the knowledge of sin*: that *every mouth* may be stopped, and *the whole world* may become guilty before God." "The law *worketh wrath.*" "The law entered, that *the offence might abound.*" "That sin by the commandment might appear *exceeding sinful.*" "As many as are of the works of the law are *under the curse.*" "We were kept under the law, shut up to the faith, which should afterwards be revealed." "Wherefore the law was our schoolmaster to bring us to Christ, that we might be justified by faith." The great work of the law was to discover what sin was: its hatefulness as accursed of God; its misery, working temporal and eternal ruin; its power, binding man down in hopeless slavery; and the need of a Divine interposition as the only hope of deliverance.

In studying the Old Covenant we ought ever to keep in mind the twofold aspect under which we have seen that Scripture represents it. It was God's grace that gave Israel the law, and wrought with the law to make it work out its purpose in individual believers and in the people as a whole. The whole of the Old Covenant was a school of grace, an elementary school, to prepare for the fulness of grace and truth in Christ Jesus. A name is generally given to an object according to its chief feature. And so the Old Covenant is called a ministration of condemnation and death, not because there was no grace in it—it had its own glory (2 Cor. 3:10-12)—but because the law with its curse was the predominating element. The combination of the two aspects we find with especial clearness in Paul's epistles. So he speaks of all who are of the works of the law as under the curse (Gal. 3:10). And then almost immediately after he speaks of the law as being our benefactor, a schoolmaster unto Christ, into whose charge, as to a tutor or governor, we had been given, till the time appointed of the Father. We are everywhere brought back to what we said above. The Old Covenant is absolutely indispensable for the preparation work it had to do; utterly insufficient to work for us a true or a full redemption.

The two great lessons God would teach us by it are very simple. The one is the lesson of SIN, the other the lesson of HOLINESS. The Old

Covenant attains its object only as it brings men to a sense of their utter sinfulness and their hopeless impotence to deliver themselves. As long as they have not learnt this, no offer of the New Covenant life can lay hold of them. As long as an intense longing for deliverance from sinning has not been wrought, they will naturally fall back into the power of the law and the flesh. The holiness which the New Covenant offers will rather terrify than attract them; the life in the spirit of bondage appears to make more allowance for sin, because obedience is declared to be impossible.

The other is the lesson of Holiness. In the New Covenant the Triune God engages to do all. He undertakes to give and keep the new heart, to give His own Spirit in it, to give the will and the power to obey and do His will. As the one demand of the first Covenant was the sense of sin, the one great demand of the New is faith that that need, created by the discipline of God's law, will be met in a Divine and supernatural way. The law cannot work out its purpose, except as it bring a man to lie guilty and helpless before the holiness of God. There the New finds him, and reveals that same God, in His grace accepting him and making him partaker of His holiness.

This book is written with a very practical purpose. Its object is to help believers to know that wonderful New Covenant of grace which God has made with them, and to lead them into the living and daily enjoyment of the blessed life it secures them. The practical lesson taught us by the fact that there was a first Covenant, that its one special work was to convince of sin, and that without it the New Covenant could not come, is just what many Christians need. At conversion they were convinced of sin by the Holy Spirit. But this had chiefly reference to the guilt of sin, and, in some degree, to its hatefulness. But a real knowledge of the power of sin, of their entire and utter impotence to cast it out, or to work in themselves what is good, is what they did not learn at once. And until they have learned this, they cannot possibly enter fully into the blessing of the New Covenant. It is when a man sees that, as little as he could raise himself from the dead, can he make or keep his own soul alive, that he becomes capable of appreciating the New Testament promise, and is made willing to wait on God to do all in him.

Do you, my reader, feel that you are not fully living in the New Covenant, that there is still somewhat of the Old-Covenant spirit of bondage in you?—do come, and let the Old Covenant finish its work in you. Accept its teaching, that all your efforts are failures. As, at conversion, you were content to fall down as a condemned, death-deserving sinner, be content now to sink down before God in the confession that, as His redeemed child, you still feel yourself utterly impotent to do and be what you see He asks of you. And begin to ask whether the New Covenant has not perhaps a provision you have never yet understood for meeting your impotence and giving you the strength to do what is well-pleasing to God. You will find the wonderful answer in the assurance that God, by His Holy Spirit, undertakes to work everything in you.

4
The New Covenant

"But this is the covenant that I will make with the house of Israel; After those days, saith the Lord, I will put My law in their inward parts, and write it in their hearts; and will be their God, and they shall be My people. And they shall teach no more every man his neighbour, Baying, Know the Lord: for they shall all know Me, from the least of them unto the greatest of them, for I will forgive their iniquity, and I will remember their sin no more" (Jeremiah 31:33-34).

ISAIAH HAS OFTEN been called the evangelical prophet, for the wonderful clearness with which he announces the coming Redeemer, both in His humiliation and suffering, and in the glory of the kingdom He was to establish. And yet it was given to Jeremiah, in this passage, and to Ezekiel, in the parallel one, to foretell what would actually be the outcome of the Redeemer's work and the essential character of the salvation He was to effect, with a distinctness which is nowhere found in the older prophet. In words which the New Testament (Hebrews 8) takes as the divinely inspired revelation of what the New Covenant is of which Christ is the Mediator, God's plan is revealed, and we are shown what it is that He will do in us, to make us fit and worthy of being the people of which He is the God. Through the whole of the Old Covenant there was always one trouble: man's heart was not right with God. In the New Covenant the evil is to be remedied. Its central promise is a heart delighting in God's law and capable of knowing and holding fellowship with Him. Let us mark the fourfold blessing spoken of.

1. *"I will put My law in their inward parts, and write it in their hearts."* Let us understand this well. In our inward parts, or in our heart, there are no separate chambers in which the law can be put, while the rest of the heart can be given up to other things; the heart is a unity. Nor are the inward parts and the heart like a house, which can be filled with things of an entirely different nature from what the walls are made of, without

any living organic connection. No; the inward parts, the heart, are the disposition, the love, the will, the life. Nothing can be put into the heart, and especially by God, without entering and taking possession of it, without securing its affection and controlling its whole being. And this is what God undertakes to do in the power of His divine life and operation, to breathe the very spirit of His law into and through the whole inward being. "I will put it into their inward parts, and write it in their hearts." At Sinai the tables of the Covenant, with the law written on them, were of stone, as a lasting substance. It is easy to know what that means. The stone was wholly set apart for this one thing—to carry and show this Divine writing. The writing and the stone were inseparably connected. And so the heart in which God gets His way, and writes His law in power, lives only and wholly to carry that writing, and is unchangeably identified with it. So alone can God realise His purpose in creation, and have His child of one mind and one spirit with Himself, delighting in doing His will. When the Old Covenant with the law graven on stone had done its work in the discovering and condemning of SIN, the New Covenant would give in its stead the life of obedience and true holiness of heart. The whole of the Covenant blessing centres in this—the heart being put right and fitted to know God: "I will give them *an heart to know Me,* that I am the Lord; and they shall be My people, and I will be their God; for they shall return unto Me *with their whole heart"* (Jer. 24:7).

2. *"And I will be their God, and they shall be My people."* Do not pass these words lightly. They occur chiefly in Jeremiah and Ezekiel in connection with the promise of the everlasting Covenant. They express the very highest experience of the Covenant relationship. It is only when His people learn to love and obey His law, when their heart and life are together wholly devoted to Him and His will, that He can be to them the altogether inconceivable blessing which these words express, *"I will be your God."* All I am and have as God shall be yours. All you can need or wish for in a God, I will be to you. In the fullest meaning of the word, I, the Omnipresent, will be ever present with you, in all My grace and love. I, the Almighty One, will each moment work all in you by My

mighty power. I, the Thrice-Holy One, will reveal My sanctifying life within you. I will be your God. *And ye shall be My people,* saved and blessed, ruled and guided and provided for by Me, known and seen to be indeed the people of the Holy One, the God of glory. Only let us give our hearts time to meditate and wait for the Holy Spirit to work in us all that these words mean.

3. *"And they shall teach no more every man his neighbour, and every man his brother, saying, Know the Lord, for they shall all know Me, from the least of them unto the greatest of them, saith the Lord."* Individual personal fellowship with God, for the feeblest and the least, is to be the wonderful privilege of every member of the New Covenant people. Each one will know the Lord. That does not mean the knowledge of the mind,—that is not the equal privilege of all, and that in itself may hinder the fellowship more than help it,—but with that knowledge which means appropriation and assimilation, and which is eternal life. As the Son knew the Father because He was one with Him and dwelt in Him, the child of God will receive by the Holy Spirit that spiritual illumination which will make God to him the One he knows best, because he loves Him most and lives in Him. The promise, "They shall be all taught of God," will be fulfilled by the Holy Spirit's teaching. God will speak to each out of His Word what he needs to know.

4. *"For I will forgive their iniquities, and I will remember their sin no more."* The word *for* shows that this is the reason of all that precedes. Because the blood of this New Covenant was of such infinite worth, and its Mediator and High Priest in heaven of such Divine power, there is promised in it such a Divine blotting out of sin that God cannot remember it. It is this entire blotting out of sin that cleanses and sets us free from its power, so that God can write His law in our hearts, and show Himself in power as our God, and by His Spirit reveal to us His deep things—the deep mystery of Himself and His love. It is the atonement and redemption of Jesus Christ wrought without us and for us, that has removed every obstacle and made it meet for God, and made us meet, that the law in the heart, and the claim on our God, and

the knowledge of Him, should now be our daily life and our eternal portion.

Here we now have the Divine summary of the New Covenant inheritance. The last-named blessing, the pardon of sin, is the first in order, the root of all. The second, having God as our God, and the third, the Divine teaching, are the fruit. The tree itself that grows on this root, and bears such fruit, is what is named first—the law in the heart.[2]

The central demand of the Old Covenant, Obey My voice, and I will be your God, has now been met. With the law written in the heart, He can be our God, and we shall be His people. Perfect harmony with God's will, holiness in heart and life, is the only thing that can satisfy God's heart or ours. And it is this the New Covenant gives in Divine power, "I will *give them an heart* to know Me; and I will be their God, and they shall be My people; for they shall turn to Me *with their whole heart."* It is on the state of the heart, it is on the new heart, as *given by God,* that the New Covenant life hinges.

But why, if all this is meant to be literally and exactly true of God's people, why do we see so little of this life, experience so little in ourselves? There is but one answer: Because of your unbelief! We have spoken of the relation of God and man in creation as what the New Covenant is meant to make possible and real. But the law cannot be repealed that God will not compel. He can only fulfil His purpose as the heart is willing and accepts His offer. In the New Covenant all is of faith. Let us turn away from what human wisdom and human experience may say, and ask God Himself to teach us what His Covenant means. If we persevere in this prayer in a humble and teachable spirit, we can count most certainly on its promise: "They shall no more every man teach his neighbour: Know the Lord, for they shall all know Me." *The teaching of God Himself, by the Holy Spirit, to make us understand what He says to us in His Word, is our Covenant right.* Let us count upon it. It is only by a God-given faith that we can appropriate these God-given promises. And it is only by a God-given teaching and inward illumination that we can see their meaning, so as to believe them. When God teaches us the

_____

[2] On the law written in the heart, see Note B.

meaning of His promises in a heart yielded to His Holy Spirit, then alone we can believe and receive them in a power which makes them a reality in our life.

But is it really possible, amid the wear and tear of daily life, to walk in the experience of these blessings? Are they really meant for all God's children? Let us rather ask the question, Is it possible for God to do what He has promised? The one part of the promise we believe—the complete and perfect pardon of sin. Why should we not believe the other part—the law written in the heart, and the direct Divine fellowship and teaching? We have been so accustomed to separate what God has joined together, the objective, outward work of His Son, and the subjective, inward work of His Spirit, that we consider the glory of the New Covenant above the Old to consist chiefly in the redeeming work of Christ for us, and not equally in the sanctifying work of the Spirit in us. It is owing to this ignorance and unbelief of the indwelling of the Holy Spirit, as the power through whom God fulfils the New Covenant promises, that we do not really expect them to be made true to us.

Do let us turn our hearts away from all past experience of failure, *as caused by nothing but unbelief;* do let us admit fully and heartily, what failure has taught us, the absolute impossibility of even a regenerate man walking in God's law in his own strength, and then turn our hearts quietly and trustfully to our own Covenant God. Let us hear *what* He says He will do for us, and believe Him; let us rest on His unchangeable faithfulness and the surety of the Covenant, on His Almighty power and the Holy Spirit working in us; and let us give up ourselves to Him as our God. He will prove that what He has done for us in Christ is not one whit more wonderful than what He will do in us every day by the Spirit of Christ.

5

The Two Covenants: In Christian Experience

"These women are two covenants: one from Mount Sinai, bearing children unto bondage, which is Hagar. Now this Hagar answereth to Jerusalem that now is, for she is in bondage with her children. But the Jerusalem which is above is free, which is our mother. So then, brethren, we are not children of the bondwoman, but of the free. With freedom did Christ set us free. Stand fast, therefore, and be not entangled again in a yoke of bondage" (Galatians 4:24-31; 5:1).

THE HOUSE OF ABRAHAM was the Church of God of that age. The division in his house, one son, his own son, but born after the flesh, the other after the promise, was a divinely-ordained manifestation of the division there would be in all ages between the children of the bondwoman, those who served God in the spirit of bondage, and those who were children of the free, and served Him in the Spirit of His Son. The passage teaches us what the whole Epistle confirms: that the Galatians had become entangled with a yoke of bondage, and were not standing fast in the freedom with which Christ makes free indeed. Instead of living in the New Covenant, in the Jerusalem which is from above, in the liberty which the Holy Spirit gives, their whole walk proved that, though Christians, they were of the Old Covenant, which bringeth forth children unto bondage. The passage teaches us the great truth, which it is of the utmost consequence for us to apprehend thoroughly, that a man, with a measure of the knowledge and experience of the grace of God, may prove; by a legal spirit, that he is yet practically, to a large extent, under the Old Covenant. And it will show us, with wonderful clearness, what the proofs are of the absence of the true New Covenant life.

A careful study of the Epistle shows us that the difference between the two Covenants is seen in three things. *The law and its works* is contrasted with the hearing of faith, *the flesh and its religion* with the flesh crucified, *the impotence to good* with a walk in the liberty and the power of the Spirit. May the Holy Spirit reveal to us this twofold life.

The first antithesis we find in Paul's words, "Received ye the Spirit by the works of the law, or the hearing of faith?" These Galatians had indeed been born into the New Covenant; they had received the Holy Spirit. But they had been led away by Jewish teachers, and, though they had been justified by faith, they were seeking to be sanctified by works; they were looking for the maintenance and the growth of their Christian life to the observance of the law. They had not understood that, equally with the beginning, the progress of the Divine life is alone by faith, day by day receiving its strength from Christ alone; that in Jesus Christ nothing avails but faith working by love.

Almost every believer makes the same mistake as the Galatian Christians. Very few learn at conversion at once that it is only by faith that we stand, and walk, and live. They have no conception of the meaning of Paul's teaching about being dead to the law, freed from the law—about the freedom with which Christ makes us free. "As many as are led by the Spirit are not under the law." Regarding the law as a Divine ordinance for our direction, they consider themselves prepared and fitted by conversion to take up the fulfilment of the law as a natural duty. They know not that, in the New Covenant, the law written in the heart needs an unceasing faith in a Divine power, to enable us by a Divine power to keep it. They cannot understand that it is not to the law, but to a Living Person, that we are now bound, and that our obedience and holiness are only possible by the unceasing faith in His power ever working in us. It is only when this is seen, that we are prepared truly to live in the New Covenant.

The second word, that reveals the Old Covenant spirit, is the word "flesh." Its contrast is, the flesh crucified. Paul asks: "Are ye so foolish? Having begun in the Spirit, are ye made perfect in the flesh?" Flesh means our sinful human nature. At his conversion the Christian has generally no conception of the terrible evil of his nature, and the subtlety with which it offers itself to take part in the service of God. It may be most willing and diligent in God's service for a time; it may devise numberless observances for making His worship pleasing and attractive; and yet this may be all only what Paul calls "making a fair show in the flesh," "glorying in the flesh," in man's will and man's efforts. This power of the religious flesh is one of the great marks of the Old Covenant religion; it misses the deep humility and spirituality of the true worship of God—a heart and life entirely dependent upon Him.

The proof that our religion is very much that of the religious flesh, is that the sinful flesh will be found to flourish along with it. It was thus with the Galatians. While they were making a fair show in the flesh, and glorying in it, their daily life was full of bitterness and envy and hatred, and other sins. They were biting and devouring one another. Religious flesh and sinful flesh are one: no wonder that, with a great deal of religion, temper and selfishness and worldliness are so often found side by side. The religion of the flesh cannot conquer sin.

What a contrast to the religion of the New Covenant! What is the place the flesh has there? "They that are Christ's have *crucified the flesh,* with its desires and affections." Scripture speaks of the will of the flesh, the mind of the flesh, the lust of the flesh; all this the true believer has seen to be condemned and crucified in Christ: he has given it over to the death. He not only accepts the Cross, with its bearing of the curse, and its redemption from it, as his entrance into life; he glories in it as his only power day by day to overcome the flesh and the world. "I am crucified with Christ." "God forbid that I should glory save in the cross of my Lord Jesus Christ, by which I am crucified to the world." Even as nothing less than the death of Christ was needed to inaugurate the New Covenant, and the resurrection life that animates it, there is no entrance into the true New Covenant life other than by a partaking of that death.

"Fallen from grace." This is a third word that describes the condition of these Galatians in that bondage in which they were really impotent to all true good. Paul is not speaking of a final falling away here, for he still addresses them as Christians, but of their having wandered from that walk in the way of enabling and sanctifying grace, in which a Christian can get the victory over sin. As long as grace is principally connected with pardon and the entrance to the Christian life, the flesh is the only power in which to serve and work. But when we know what exceeding abundance of grace has been provided, and how God "makes all grace abound, that we may abound to all good works," we know that, as it is by faith, so too it is by grace alone that we stand a single moment or take a single step.

The contrast to this life of impotence and failure is found in the one word, "the Spirit." "If ye be led of the Spirit, ye are not under the law," with its demand on your own strength. "Walk in the Spirit, and ye shall not"—a definite, certain promise—"ye shall not fulfil the lusts of the flesh." The Spirit gives liberty from the law, from the flesh, from sin. "The fruit of the Spirit is love, peace, joy." Of the New Covenant promise, "I will put *My Spirit* within you, and *I will cause* you to walk in My statutes, and *ye shall keep* My judgments," the Spirit is the centre and the sum. He is the power of the supernatural life of true obedience and holiness.

And what would have been the course that the Galatians would have taken if they had accepted this teaching of St. Paul? As they hear his question, "Now that ye have come to know God, how turn ye back again into the weak and beggarly rudiments, whereunto ye desire to be in bondage again?" they would have felt that there was but one course. Nothing else could help them but at once to turn back again to the path they had left. At the point where they had left it, they could enter again. With any one of them who wished to do so, this turning away from the Old Covenant legal spirit, and the renewed surrender to the Mediator of the New Covenant, could be the act of a moment—one single step. As the light of the New Covenant promise dawned upon him, and he saw how Christ was to be all, and faith all, and the Holy Spirit in the heart all, and the faithfulness of a Covenant-keeping God all in all, he would feel that he had but one thing to do—in utter impotence to yield himself to God, and in simple faith to count upon Him to perform what He had spoken. In Christian experience there may be still the Old Covenant life of bondage and failure. In Christian experience there may be a life that gives way entirely to the New Covenant grace and spirit. In Christian experience, when the true vision has been received of what the New Covenant means, a faith that rests fully on the Mediator of the New Covenant can enter at once into the life which the Covenant secures.

I cannot too earnestly beg all believers who long to know to the utmost what the grace of God can work in them, to study carefully the question as to whether the acknowledgment that our being in the bondage of the Old Covenant is the reason of our failure, and whether a clear insight into the possibility of an entire change in our relation to God, is not what is needed to give us the help we seek. We may be seeking for our growth in a more diligent use of the means of grace, and a more earnest striving to live in accordance with God's will, and yet entirely fail. The reason is, that there is a secret root of evil which must be removed. That root is the spirit of bondage, the legal spirit of self-effort, which hinders that humble faith that knows that God will work all, and yields to Him to do it. That spirit may be found amidst very great zeal for God's service, and very earnest prayer for His grace; it does not enjoy the rest of faith, and cannot overcome sin, because it does not stand in the liberty with which Christ has made us free, and does not know that where the Spirit of the Lord is, there is liberty. There the soul can say: "The law of the Spirit of life in Christ Jesus *hath made me free* from the law of sin and death." When once we admit heartily, not only that there are failings in our life, but that there is something radically wrong that can be changed, we shall turn with a new interest, with a deeper confession of ignorance and impotence, with a hope that looks to God alone for teaching and strength, to find that in the New Covenant there is an actual provision for every need.

6

The Everlasting Covenant

"They shall be My people, and I will be their God. And I will make an everlasting covenant with them, that *I will not turn away from them*, to do them good; but *I will put My fear in their hearts, that they shall not depart from Me.*" (Jeremiah 32:38, 40).

"A new heart also will I give you, and a new spirit will I put within you: and I will take the stony heart out of your flesh, and I will give you an heart of flesh. And I will put my Spirit within you, *and cause you to walk in My statutes*, and *ye shall keep* My judgments, and do them. Moreover, I will make a covenant of peace with them: it shall be an everlasting covenant with them." (Ezekiel 36:26-27; 37:26).

W E HAVE HAD THE WORDS of the institution of the New Covenant. Let us listen to the further teaching we have concerning it in Jeremiah and Ezekiel, where God speaks of it as an everlasting Covenant.

In every covenant there are two parties. And the very foundation of a covenant rests on the thought that each party is to be faithful to the part it has undertaken to perform. Unfaithfulness on either side breaks the covenant.

It was thus with the Old Covenant. God had said to Israel, *Obey My voice, and I will be your God* (Jer. 7:23; 11:4). These simple words contained the whole Covenant. And when Israel disobeyed, the Covenant was broken. The question of Israel being able or not able to obey was not taken into consideration: disobedience forfeited the privileges of the Covenant.

If a New Covenant were to be made, and if that was to be better than the Old, this was the one thing to be provided for. No New Covenant could be of any profit unless provision were made for securing obedience. Obedience there must be. God as Creator could never take His creatures into His favour and fellowship, except they obeyed Him. The thing would have been an impossibility. If the New

34

Covenant is to be better than the Old, if it is to be an everlasting Covenant, never to be broken, it must make some sufficient provision for securing the obedience of the Covenant people.

And this is indeed the glory of the New Covenant, the glory that excelleth, that this provision has been made. In a way that no human thought could have devised, by a stipulation that never entered into any human covenant, by an undertaking in which God's infinite condescension and power and faithfulness are to be most wonderfully exhibited, by a supernatural mystery of Divine wisdom and grace, the New Covenant provides a guarantee, not only for God's faithfulness, *but for man's too!* And this in no other way than by God Himself undertaking to secure man's part as well as His own. Do try and get hold of this.

It is just because this, the essential part of the New Covenant, so exceeds and confounds all human thoughts of what a covenant means, that Christians, from the Galatians downwards, have not been able to see and believe what the New Covenant really means. They have thought that human unfaithfulness was a factor permanently to be reckoned with as something utterly unconquerable and incurable, and that the possibility of a life of obedience, with the witness from within of a good conscience, and from above of God's pleasure, was not to be expected. They have therefore sought to stir the mind to its utmost by arguments and motives, and never realised how the Holy Spirit is to be the unceasing, universal, all-sufficient worker of everything that has to be wrought by the Christian.

Let us beseech God earnestly that He would reveal to us by the Holy Spirit the things that He hath prepared for them that love Him; things that have not entered into the heart of man; the wonderful life of the New Covenant. All depends upon our knowledge of what God will work in us. Listen to what God says in Jeremiah of the two parts of His everlasting Covenant, shortly after He announced the New Covenant, and in further elucidation of it. The central thought of that, *that the heart is to be put right,* is here reiterated and confirmed. "I will make an everlasting covenant with them, *that I will not turn away from them, to do them good."* That is, God will be unchangeably faithful. He will not turn from us. "But *I will put My fear into their heart, that they shall not depart from Me.*" This is the second half: Israel will be unchangeably faithful too. And that because God will so put His fear in their heart, that they shall not depart from Him. *As little as God will turn from them, will they depart from Him!* As faithfully as He undertakes for the fulfilment of His part, will He undertake for the fulfilment of their part, that they shall not depart from Him!

Listen to God's word in Ezekiel, in regard to one of the terms of His Covenant of peace, His everlasting Covenant (Ezek. 34:25; 36:27; 37:26): "I will put My Spirit within you, and *cause you to walk in My statutes,* and *ye shall keep* My judgments, and do them." In the Old Covenant we have nothing of this sort. You have, on the contrary, from the story of the golden calf and the breaking of the Tables of the Covenant onward, the sad fact of continual departure from God. We find God longing for what He would so fain have seen, but was not to be found. "O that there were such an heart in them, that they would fear Me, and keep all My commandments always" (Deut. 5:29). We find throughout the Book of Deuteronomy, a thing without parallel in the history of any religion or religious lawgiver, that Moses most distinctly prophesies their forsaking of God, with the terrible curses and dispersion that would come upon them. It is only at the close of his threatenings (Deut. 30:6) that he gives the promise of the new time that would come: "The Lord thy God will circumcise thine heart, to love the Lord thy God with all thine heart, and with all thy soul, and *thou shalt obey* the voice of the Lord thy God." The whole Old Covenant was dependent on man's faithfulness: "The Lord thy God *keepeth covenant* with them *that keep* His commandments." God's keeping the Covenant availed little, if man did not keep it. Nothing could help man until the *"If ye shall diligently keep"* of the law was replaced by the word of promise, "I will put My Spirit in you, and *ye shall keep* My judgments, and do them." The one supreme difference of the New Covenant; the one thing for which the Mediator, and the Blood, and the Spirit were given; the one fruit God sought and Himself engaged to bring forth was this: a heart filled with His fear and love, a heart to cleave unto Him and not depart from Him, a heart in which His Spirit and His law dwells, a heart that delights to do His will.

Here is the inmost secret of the New Covenant. It deals with the heart of man in a way of Divine power. It not only appeals to the heart by every motive of fear or love, of duty or gratitude. That the law also did. But it reveals God Himself, cleansing our heart and making it new, changing it entirely from a stony heart into a heart of flesh, a tender, living, loving heart, putting His Spirit within it, and so, by His Almighty Power and Love, breathing and working in it, making the promise true, *"I will cause you* to walk in My statutes, and *ye shall keep* My judgments."* A heart in perfect harmony with Himself, a life and walk in His way—God has engaged in Covenant to work this in us. He undertakes for our part in the Covenant as much as for His own.

This is nothing but the restoration of the original relation between God and the man He had made in His likeness. He was on earth to be the very image of God, because God was to live and to work all in him, and he to find his glory and blessedness in thus owing all to God. This is the exceeding glory of the New Covenant, of the Pentecostal dispensation, that by the Holy Spirit God could now again be the indwelling life of His people, and so make the promise a reality: "I will cause you to walk in My statutes."

With God's presence secured to us every moment of the day—"I will not turn away from them"; with God's "fear put into our heart" by His own Spirit, and our heart thus responding to His holy presence; with our hearts thus made right with God, we can, we shall walk in His statutes, and keep His judgments.

My brethren, the great sin of Israel under the Old Covenant, that by which they greatly grieved Him, was this: "they limited the Holy One of Israel." Under the New Covenant there is no less danger of this sin. *It makes it impossible for God to fulfil His promises.* Let us seek, above everything, for the Holy Spirit's teaching, to show us exactly what God has established the New Covenant for, that we may honour Him by believing all that His love has prepared for us.

And if we ask for the cause of the unbelief, that prevents the fulfilment of the promise, we shall find that it is not far to seek. It is, in most cases, the lack of desire for the promised blessing. In all who came to Jesus on earth the intensity of their desire for the healing they needed made them ready and glad to believe in His word. Where the law has done its full work, where the actual desire to be freed from every sin is strong, and masters the heart, the presence of the New Covenant, when once really understood, comes like bread to a famishing man. The subtle belief that it is impossible to be kept from sinning cuts away the power of accepting the promises of the everlasting Testament promise. God's Word, "I will put My fear in their heart, that *they shall not* depart from Me"; "I will put My Spirit within you, and *ye shall* keep My judgment," is understood in some feeble sense, according to our experience, and not according to what the Word and what God means. And the soul settles down into a despair, or a self-contentment, that says it can never be otherwise, and makes true conviction for sin impossible.

Let me say to every reader who would fain be able to believe fully all that God says: Cherish every whisper of the conscience and of the Spirit that convinces of sin. Whatever it be, a hasty temper, a sharp word, an unloving or impatient thought, anything of selfishness or self-will—cherish that which condemns it in you, as part of the schooling that is to bring you to Christ and the full possession of His salvation. The New Covenant is meant to meet the need for a power of not sinning, which the Old could not give. Come with that need; it will prepare and open the heart for all the everlasting Covenant secures you.

7

The New Covenant:
A Ministration of the Spirit

"Ye are an epistle of Christ, ministered by as, written not with ink, but with the Spirit of the living God; not on tables of stone, but on tables that are hearts of flesh. . . . Our sufficiency is of God; who also made us sufficient as ministers of the New Covenant; not of the letter, but of the Spirit: for the letter killeth, but the Spirit giveth life. For if the ministration of death came with glory, how shall not rather the ministration of the Spirit be with glory? For if the ministration of condemnation is glory, much rather doth the ministration of righteousness exceed in glory" (2 Corinthians 3.3, 6-10).

IN THIS WONDERFUL chapter Paul reminds the Corinthians, in speaking of his ministry among them, of what its chief characteristics were. As a ministry of the New Covenant he contrasts it, and the whole dispensation of which it is part, with that of the Old. The Old was graven in stone, the New in the heart. The Old could be written in ink, and was in the letter that killeth; the New, of the Spirit that maketh alive. The Old was a ministration of condemnation and death; the New, of righteousness and life. The Old indeed had its glory, for it was of Divine appointment, and brought its Divine blessing; but it was a glory that passed away, and had no glory by reason of the glory that excelleth, the exceeding glory of that which remaineth. With the Old there was the veil on the heart; in the New, the veil is taken away from the face and the heart, the Spirit of the Lord gives liberty, and, reflecting with unveiled face the glory of the Lord, we are changed from glory to glory, into the same image, as by the Spirit of the Lord. The glory that excelleth proved its power in this, that it not only marked the dispensation on its Divine side, but exerted its power in the heart and life of its subjects, so that it was seen in them too, as they were changed by the Spirit into Christ's image, from glory to glory.

Think a moment of the contrast. The Old Covenant was of the letter that killeth. The law came with its literal instruction, and sought by the knowledge it gave of God's will to appeal to man's fear and his love, to his natural powers of mind and conscience and will. It spoke to him as if he could obey, that it might convince him of what he did not know, that he could not obey. And so it fulfilled its mission: "The commandment which was unto life, this I found to be unto death." In the New, on the contrary, how different was everything. Instead of the letter, the Spirit that giveth life, that breathes the very life of God, the life of heaven into us. Instead of a law graven in stone, the law written in the heart, worked into the heart's affection and powers, making it one with them. Instead of the vain attempt to work from without inward, the Spirit and the law are put into the inward parts, thence to work outward in life and walk.

This passage brings into view that which is the distinctive blessing of the New Covenant. In working out our salvation God bestowed upon us two wonderful gifts. We read:

"God sent forth His Son, that He might redeem them that were under the law, that we might receive the adoption of sons. And because ye are sons, *God sent forth the Spirit of His Son* into your hearts, crying, Abba, Father."*

Here we have the two parts of God's work in salvation. The one, the more objective, what He did that we might become His children—He sent forth His Son. The second, the more subjective, what He did that we might live like His children: He sent forth the Spirit of His Son into our hearts. In the former we have the external manifestation of the work of redemption; in the other, its inward appropriation; the former for the sake of the latter. These two halves form one great whole, and may not be separated.

In the promises of the New Covenant, as we find them in Jeremiah and Ezekiel, as well as in our text and many other passages of Scripture, it is manifest that God's great object in salvation is to get possession of the heart. The heart is the real life; with the heart a man loves, and wills, and acts; the heart makes the man. God made man's heart for His own dwelling, that in it He might reveal His love and His glory. God sent Christ to accomplish a redemption by which man's heart could be won back to Him; nothing but that could satisfy God. And that is what is accomplished when the Holy Spirit makes the heart of His child what it should be. The whole work of Christ's redemption—His Atonement and Victory, His Exaltation and Intercession, His glory at the right hand of God—all these are only preparatory to what is the chief triumph of His grace: the renewal of the heart to be the temple of God. Through Christ God gives the Holy Spirit to glorify Him in the heart, by working there all that He has done and is doing for the soul.

In a great deal of our religious teaching a fear, lest we should derogate from the honour of Christ, has been alleged as the reason for giving His work for us, on the Cross or in heaven, a greater prominence than His work in our heart by the Holy Spirit. The result has been that the indwelling of the Holy Spirit, and His mighty work as the life of the heart, are very little known or experienced. If we look carefully at what the New Covenant promises mean, we shall see how the "sending forth of the Spirit of His Son into our hearts" is indeed the consummation and crown of Christ's redeeming work. Let us just think of what these promises imply.

In the Old Covenant man had failed in what he had to do. In the New, God is to do everything in him. The Old could only convict of sin. The New is to put it away and cleanse the heart from its filthiness. In the Old it was the heart that was wrong; for the New a new heart is provided, into which God puts His fear and His law and His love. The Old demanded, but failed to secure obedience; in the New, God causes us to walk in His judgments. The New is to fit man for a true holiness, a true fulfilment of the law of loving God with the whole heart, and our neighbours as ourselves, a walk truly well-pleasing to God. The New changes a man from glory to glory after the image of Christ. All because the Spirit of God's Son is given into the heart. The Old gave no power: in the New all is by the Spirit, the mighty power of God. As complete as the reign and power of Christ on the throne of heaven, is His dominion on the throne of the heart by His Holy Spirit given to us.[3]

It is as we bring all these traits of the New Covenant life together into one focus, and look at the heart of God's child as the object of this mighty redemption, that we shall begin to understand what it secures to us, and what it is that we are to expect from our Covenant God. We shall see wherein the glory of the ministration of the Spirit consists, even in this, that God can fill our heart with His love, and make it His abode.

We are accustomed to say, and truly so, that the worth of the Son of God, who came to die for us, is the measure of the worth of the soul in God's sight, and of the greatness of the work that had to be done to save it. Let us even so see that the Divine glory of the Holy Spirit, the Spirit of the Father and the Son, is the measure of God's longing to have our heart wholly for Himself, of the glory of the work that is to be wrought within us, of the power by which that work will be accomplished.

We shall see how the glory of the ministration of the Spirit is no other than the glory of the Lord, as it is not only in heaven, but resting upon us and dwelling in us, and changing us into the same image from glory to glory. The inconceivable glory of our exalted Lord in heaven has its counterpart here on earth in the exceeding glory of the Holy Spirit who glorifies Him in us, who lays His glory on us, as He changes us into His likeness.

The New Covenant has no power to save and to bless except as it is a ministration of the Spirit. That Spirit works in lesser or greater degree, as He is neglected and grieved, or yielded to and trusted. Let us honour Him, and give Him His place as the Spirit of the New Covenant, by expecting and accepting all He waits to do for us.

He is the great gift of the Covenant. His coming from heaven was the proof that the Mediator of the Covenant was on the throne in glory, and could now make us partakers of the heavenly life.

---

[3] See Note C, on George Müller.

He is the only teacher of what the Covenant means: dwelling in our heart, He wakens there the thought and the desire for what God has prepared for us.

He is the Spirit of faith, who enables us to believe the otherwise incomprehensible blessing and power in which the New Covenant works, and to claim it as our own.

He is the Spirit of grace and of power, by whom the obedience of the Covenant and the fellowship with God can be maintained without interruption.

He Himself is the Possessor and the Bearer and the Communicator of all the Covenant promises, the Revealer and the Glorifier of Jesus, its Mediator and Surety.

To believe fully in the Holy Spirit, as the present and abiding and all-comprehending gift of the New Covenant, has been to many a one an entrance into its fulness of blessing.

Begin at once, child of God, to give the Holy Spirit the place in thy religion He has in God's plan. Be still before God, and believe that He is within thee, and ask the Father to work in thee through Him. Regard thyself, thy spirit as well as thy body, with holy reverence as His temple. Let the consciousness of His holy presence and working fill thee with holy calm and fear. And be sure that all that God calls thee to be, Christ through His Spirit will work in thee.

8

The Two Covenants: The Transition

"Now the God of peace, who brought again from the dead the great Shepherd of the sheep, in the blood of the everlasting covenant, even our Lord Jesus, make you perfect in every good thing to do His will, working in us that which is well-pleasing in His sight, through Jesus Christ" (Hebrews 13:20-21).

THE TRANSITION FROM the Old Covenant to the New was not slow or gradual, but by a tremendous crisis. Nothing less than the death of Christ was the close of the Old. Nothing less than His resurrection from the dead, through the blood of the everlasting Covenant, the opening of the New. The path of preparation that led up to the crisis was long and slow; the rending of the veil, that symbolised the end of the old worship, was the work of a moment. By a death, once for all, Christ's work, as fulfiller of law and prophets, as the end of the law, was for ever finished. By a resurrection in the power of an endless life, the Covenant of Life was ushered in.

These events have an infinite significance, as revealing the character of the Covenants they are related to. The death of Christ shows the true nature of the Old Covenant. It is elsewhere called "a ministration of death" (2 Cor. 3:7). It brought forth nothing but death. It ended in death; only by death could the life that had been lived under it be brought to an end. The New was to be a Covenant of Life; it had its birth in the omnipotent resurrection power that brought Christ from the dead; its one mark and blessing is, that all it gives comes, not only as a promise, but as an experience, in the power of an endless life. The Death reveals the utter *inefficacy* and *insufficiency* of the Old; the Life brings nigh and imparts to us for ever all that the New has to offer. An insight into the completeness of the transition, as seen in Christ, prepares us for apprehending the reality of the change in our life, when, "like as Christ was raised from the dead by the glory of the Father, so we also walk in newness of life."

The complete difference between the life in the Old and the New is remarkably illustrated by a previous passage in the Epistle (Heb. 9:16). After having said that a death for the redemption of transgressions had to take place ere the New Covenant could be established, the writer adds, "Where a testament is, there must of necessity be the death of him that made it."[4] Before any heir can obtain the legacy, its first owner, the testator, must have died. The old proprietorship, the old life, must disappear entirely before the new heir, the new life, can enter upon the inheritance. Nothing but death can work the transference of the property. It is even so with Christ, with the Old and the New Covenant life, with our own deliverance from the Old and our entrance on the New. Now, having been made dead to the law by the body of Christ, we have been discharged from the law, having died to that wherein we were holden—here is the completeness of the deliverance from Christ's side; "so that we serve"—here is the completeness of the change in our experience—"in newness of the spirit, and not in oldness of the letter."

The transition, if it is to be real and whole, must take place by a death. As with Christ the Mediator of the Covenant, so with His people, the heirs of the Covenant. In Him we are dead to sin; in Him we are dead to the law. Just as Adam died to God, and we inherit a nature actually and really dead in sin, dead to God and His kingdom, so in Christ we died to sin, and inherit a nature actually dead to sin and its dominion. It is when the Holy Spirit reveals and makes real to us this death to sin and to the law too, as the one condition of a life to God, that the transition from the Old to the New Covenant can be fully realised in us. The Old was, and was meant to be, a "ministration of death"; until it has completely done its work in us there is no complete discharge from its power. The man who sees that self is incurably evil and must die; who gives self utterly to death as he sinks before God in utter impotence and the surrender to His working; who consents to death with Christ on the cross as his desert, and in faith accepts it as his

---

[4] The Greek word for "covenant" and "testament" is the same. This is the only passage where the allusion to a testator makes the meaning *testament* a necessity. Everywhere else the Revised Version has rightly used "covenant."

only deliverance; he alone is prepared to be led by the Holy Spirit into the full enjoyment of the New Covenant life. He will learn to understand how completely death makes an end to all self-effort, and how, as he lives in Christ to God, everything henceforth is to be the work of God Himself.

See how beautifully our text brings out this truth, that just as much as Christ's resurrection out of death was the work of God Himself, is our life equally to be wholly God's own work too. Not more direct and wonderful than was in Christ the transition from death to life, is to be in us the experience of what the New Covenant life is to bring. Notice the subject of the two verses. In ver. 20 we have what God *has done* in raising Christ from the dead; in ver. 21, what God *is to do in us*, working in us what is pleasing to Him.

(20) "The God of peace, who brought from the dead that great Shepherd of the sheep, even our Lord Jesus, (21) Make you perfect in every good thing to do His will, working in you that which is pleasing in His sight, through Jesus Christ."

We have the name of our Lord Jesus twice. In the first case it refers to what God has done to Christ for us, raising Him; in the second, to what God is doing through Christ in us, working His pleasure in us. Because it is the same God continuing in us the work He began in Christ, it is in us just what it was in Christ. In Christ's death we see Him in utter impotence allowing and counting upon God to work all and give Him life. God wrought the wonderful transition. In us we see the same; it is only as we give ourself unto that death too, as we entirely cease from self and its works, as we lie as in the grave waiting for God to work all, that the God of resurrection life can work in us all His good pleasure.

It was "through the blood of the everlasting Covenant," with its atonement for sin, and its destruction of sin's power, that God effected that resurrection. It is through that same blood that we are redeemed and freed from the power of sin, and made partakers of Christ's resurrection life. The more we study the New Covenant, the more we shall see that its one aim is to restore man, out of the Fall, to the life in

God for which he was created. It does this first, by delivering him from the power of sin in Christ's death, and then by taking possession of his heart, his life, for God to work all in him by the Holy Spirit. The whole argument of the Epistle to the Hebrews as to the Old and New Covenants is here summed up in these concluding verses. Just as He raised Christ from the dead, the God of the everlasting Covenant can and will now make you perfect in every good thing to do His will, working in you that which is well-pleasing in His sight through Jesus Christ. Your doing His will is the object of creation and redemption. God's working it all in you is what redemption has made possible. The Old Covenant of law and effort and failure has ended in condemnation and death. The New Covenant is coming to give, in all whom the law has slain and brought to bow in their utter impotence, the law written in the heart, the Spirit dwelling there, and God working all, both to will and to do, through Jesus Christ.

Oh for a Divine revelation that the transition from Christ's death, in its impotence, to His life in God's power, is the image, the pledge, the power of our transition out of the Old Covenant, when it has slain us, to the New, with God working in us all in all!

The transition from Old to New, as effected in Christ, was sudden. Is it so in the believer? Not always. In us it depends upon a revelation. There have been cases in which a believer, sighing and struggling against the yoke of bondage, has in one moment had it given to him to see what a complete salvation the New Covenant brings to the heart and the inner life, through the ministration of the Spirit, and by faith he has entered at once into his rest. There have been other cases in which, gradual as the dawn of day, the light of God has risen upon the heart. God's offer of entrance into the enjoyment of our New Covenant privileges is always urgent and immediate. Every believer is a child of the New Covenant, and heir of all its promises. The death of the Testator gives him full right to immediate possession. God longs to bring us into the land of promise; let us not come short through unbelief.

May God reveal to us the difference between the two lives under the Old and the New; the resurrection power of the New, with God working all in us; the power of the transition secured to us in death with Christ and life in Him. And may He teach us at once to trust Christ Jesus for a full participation in all the New Covenant secures.

There may be someone who can hardly believe that such a mighty change in his life is within his reach, and yet who would fain know what he is to do if there is to be any hope of his attaining it. I have just said, the death of the testator gives the heir immediate right to the inheritance. And yet the heir, if he be a minor, does not enter on the possession. A term of years ends the stage of minority on earth, and he is no longer under guardians. In the spiritual life the state of pupilage ends, not with the expiry of years, but the moment the minor proves his fitness for being made free from the law, by accepting the liberty there is in Christ Jesus. The transition, as with the Old Testament, as with Christ, as with the disciples, comes when the time is fulfilled and all things are now ready.

But what is one to do who is longing to be thus made ready? Accept your death to sin in Christ, and act it out. Acknowledge the sentence of death on everything that is of nature: take and keep the place before God of utter unworthiness and helplessness; sink down before Him in humility, meekness, patience, and resignation to His will and mercy.[5]

Fix your heart upon the great and mighty God, who in His grace will work in you above what you can ask or think, and will make you a monument of His mercy. Believe that every blessing of the Covenant of grace is yours; by the death of the Testator you are entitled to it all—and on that faith act, knowing that all is yours. The new heart is yours, the law written in the heart is yours, the Holy Spirit, the seal of the Covenant, is yours. Act on the faith, and count upon God as Faithful and Able, and oh! so Loving, to reveal in you, to make true in you, all the power and glory of His everlasting Covenant.

---

[5] If you would understand the full meaning of this sentence and know how to practise its teaching, consult a little book just published, *Dying to Self: A Golden Dialogue.* By William Law, with Notes by Rev. Andrew Murray (Nisbet *&* Co.).

9

The Blood of the Covenant

"Behold the blood of the covenant, which the Lord hath made with you" (Exodus 24:8; Hebrews 9:20).

"This cup is the new covenant in My blood" (1 Corinthians 11:25; Matthew 26:28).

"The blood of the covenant, wherewith he was sanctified" (Hebrews 10:29).

"The blood of the everlasting covenant" (Hebrews 13:21).

THE BLOOD IS ONE of the strangest, the deepest, the mightiest, and the most heavenly of the thoughts of God. It lies at the very root of both Covenants, but specially of the New Covenant. The difference between the two Covenants is the difference between the blood of beasts, and the blood of the Lamb of God! The power of the New Covenant has no lesser measure than the worth of the blood of the Son of God! Your Christian experience ought to know of no standard of peace with God, and purity from sin and power over the world, than the blood of Christ can give! If we would enter truly and fully into all the New Covenant is meant to be to us, let us beseech God to reveal to us the worth and the power of the blood of the Covenant, the precious blood of Christ!

The First Covenant was not brought in without blood. There could be no Covenant of friendship between a holy God and sinful men without atonement and reconciliation; and no atonement without a death as the penalty of sin. God spake: "I have given you the blood upon the altar to make an atonement for your souls; for it is the blood that maketh an atonement for the soul." The blood shed in death meant the death of a sacrifice slain for sin of man; the blood sprinkled on the altar meant that vicarious death accepted of God for the sinful one. No forgiveness, no covenant without blood-shedding.

49

All this was but type and shadow of what was one day to become a mysterious reality. What no thought of man or angel could have conceived, what even now passeth all understanding, the Eternal Son of God took flesh and blood, and then shed that blood as the blood of the New Covenant, not merely to ratify it, but to open the way for it and to make it possible. Yea, more, to be, in time and eternity, the living power by which entrance into the Covenant was to be obtained, and all life in it be secured. Until we learn to form an expectation of a life in the New Covenant, according to the inconceivable worth and power of the blood of God's Son, we never can have even an insight into the entirely supernatural and heavenly life that a child of God may live. Let us think for a moment on the threefold light in which Scripture teaches us to regard it.

In the passage from Hebrews 9:15 we read:

"For this cause Christ is the Mediator of a new covenant, that a death having taken place for the redemption of the transgressions that were under the first covenant, they that have been called may receive the promise of the eternal inheritance."

The sins of the ages of the First Covenant, which had only figuratively been atoned for, had gathered up before God. A death was needed for the redemption of these. In that death and blood-shedding of the Lamb of God not only were these atoned for, but the power of all sin was for ever broken.

The blood of the New Covenant is redemption blood, a purchase price and ransom from the power of Sin and the Law. In any purchase made on earth the transference of property from the old owner to the new is complete. Its worth may be ever so great and the hold on it ever so strong, if the price be paid, it is gone for ever from him who owned it. The hold sin had on us was terrible. No thought can realise its legitimate claim on us under God's law, its awful tyrant power in enslaving us. But the blood of God's Son has been paid.

"Ye were redeemed, not with corruptible things as silver and gold, from your vain manner of life handed down from your fathers, but with precious blood, as of a lamb without spot, even the blood of Christ."

We have been rescued, ransomed, redeemed out of our old natural life, under the power of sin, utterly and eternally. Sin has not the slightest claim on us, nor the slightest power over us, except as our ignorance or unbelief or half-heartedness allows it to have dominion. Our New Covenant birthright is to stand in the freedom with which Christ has made us free. Until the soul sees, and accepts and desires, and claims the redemption and the liberty which has the blood of the Son of God for its purchase price, and its measure, and its security, it never can fully live the New Covenant life.

As wonderful as the blood-shedding for our redemption is the blood-sprinkling for our cleansing. Here is indeed another of the spiritual mysteries of the New Covenant, which lose their power when understood in human wisdom, without the ministration of the Spirit of life. When Scripture speaks of "having our hearts sprinkled from an evil conscience," of "the blood of Christ cleansing our conscience," of our singing here on earth (Rev. 1:5), "To Him that washed us from our sins in His blood," it brings this mighty, quickening blood of the Lamb into direct contact with our hearts. It gives the assurance that that blood, in its infinite worth, in its Divine sin-cleansing power, can keep us clean in our walk in the sight and the light of God. It is as this blood of the New Covenant is known, and trusted, and waited for, and received from God, in its Divine mighty operation in the heart, that we shall begin to believe that the blessed promise of a New Covenant life and walk can be fulfilled.

There is one more thing Scripture teaches concerning this blood of the New Covenant. When the Jews contrasted Moses with our Lord Jesus, He spake: "Except ye eat the flesh of the Son of man, and drink His blood, ye have not life in yourselves. He that eateth My flesh, and drinketh My blood, abideth in Me, and I in him." As if the redeeming, and sprinkling, and washing, and sanctifying does not sufficiently express the intense inwardness of its action and its power to permeate our whole being, the drinking of this precious blood is declared to be indispensable to having life. If we would enter deep into the Spirit and power of the New Covenant, let us, by the Holy Spirit, drink deep of this cup—the cup of the New Covenant in His blood.

On account of sin there could be no covenant between man and God without blood, and no New Covenant without the blood of the Son of God. As the cleansing away of sins was the first condition in making a covenant, so it is equally the first condition of an entrance into it. It has ever been found that a deeper appropriation of the blessings of the Covenant must be preceded by a new and deeper cleansing from sin. We know how in Ezekiel the words about God's causing us to walk in His statutes are preceded by *"From all your filthiness will I cleanse you."* And then later we read (37:23, 25),

"Neither shall they defile themselves any more with any of their transgressions; *I will cleanse them. So* shall they be My people, and I will be their God. Moreover, I will make a Covenant of peace with them; it shall be an everlasting Covenant with them."

The confession and casting away, and the cleansing away of sin in the blood, are the indispensable, but all-sufficient, preparation for a life in everlasting Covenant with God.

Many feel that they do not understand or realise this wonderful power of the blood. Much thought does not help them; even prayer does not appear to bring the light they seek. The blood of Christ is a Divine mystery that passes all thought. Like every spiritual and heavenly blessing, this too, but this especially, needs to be imparted to us by the Holy Spirit. It was through the Eternal Spirit that Christ offered the sacrifice in which the blood was shed. The blood had the life of Christ, the life of the Spirit, in it. The outpouring of the blood for us was to prepare the way for the outpouring of the Spirit on us. It is the Holy Spirit, and He alone, who can minister the blood of the everlasting Covenant in power. Just as He leads the soul to the initial faith in the pardon that blood has purchased, and the peace it gives, He leads further to the knowledge and experience of its cleansing power. Here again, too, by faith—a faith in a heavenly power, of which it does not fully understand, nor cannot define, the action, but of which it knows that it is an operation of God's mighty power, and effects a cleansing that does give a clean heart,—a clean heart, first known and accepted by the same faith, apart from signs or feelings, apart from sense or reason, and then experienced in the joy and the fellowship with God it brings. Oh! let us believe in the blood of the everlasting Covenant, and the cleansing the Holy Spirit ministers. Let us believe in the ministration of the Holy Spirit, until our whole life in the New Covenant becomes entirely His work, to the glory of the Father and of Christ.

The blood of the Covenant, O mystery of mysteries! O grace above all grace! O mighty power of God, opening the way into the holiest, and into our hearts, and into the New Covenant, where the Holy One and our heart meets! Let us ask God much, by His Holy Spirit, to make us know what it is and works.

10
Jesus, the Mediator of the New Covenant

"I give thee for a covenant of the people" (Isaiah 42:6; 49:8).

"The Lord shall suddenly come to His temple, even the Messenger of the covenant, whom ye delight in" (Malachi 3:1).

"Jesus was made Surety of a better covenant" (Hebrews 7:22).

"The Mediator of the Better Covenant, established upon better promises. . . . The Mediator of the New Covenant. . . . Ye are come to Jesus, the Mediator of the New Covenant" (Hebrews 8:6; 9:15; 12:24).

WE HAVE HERE FOUR titles given to our Lord Jesus in connection with the New Covenant. He is Himself called a Covenant. The union between God and man, which the Covenant aims at, was wrought out in Him personally; in Him the reconciliation between the human and Divine was perfectly effected; in Him His people find the Covenant with all its blessings; He is all that God has to give, and is the assurance that it is given. . . . He is called the Messenger of the Covenant, because He came to establish and to proclaim it. . . . He is the Surety of the Covenant, not only because He paid our debt, but as He is Surety to us for God, that God will fulfil His part; and Surety for us with God, that we will fulfil our part. . . . And He is Mediator of the Covenant, because as the Covenant was established in His atoning blood, is administered and applied by Him, is entered upon alone by faith in Him, so it is experimentally known only through the power of His resurrection life, and His never-ceasing intercession. All these names point to the one truth, that in the New Covenant Christ is all in all.

The subject is so large that it would be impossible to enter upon all the various aspects of this precious truth. Christ's work in atonement and intercession, in His bestowal of pardon and the Holy Spirit, in His daily communication of grace and strength, are truths which lie at the very foundation of the faith of Christians. We need not speak of them here. What specially needs to be made clear to many is how, by faith in Christ as the Mediator of the New Covenant, we actually have access to and enter into the enjoyment of all its promised blessings. We have already seen, in studying the New Covenant, how all these blessings culminate in the one thing—that the heart of man is to be put right, as the only possible way of his living in the favour of God, and God's love finding its satisfaction in him. That he is to receive a heart to fear God, to love God with all his strength, to obey God, and to keep all His statutes. All that Christ did and does has this for its aim; all the higher blessings of peace and fellowship flow from this. In this God's saving power and love find the highest proof of their triumph over sin. Nothing so reveals the grace of God, the power of Jesus Christ, the reality of salvation, the blessedness of the New Covenant, as the heart of a believer, where sin once abounded, with grace now abounding more exceedingly within it.

I do not know how I can better set forth the glory of our Blessed Lord Jesus as He accomplishes this, the real object of His redeeming work, and as He takes entire possession of the heart He has bought and won and washed as a dwelling for His Father, than by pointing out the place He takes, and the work He does, in the case of a soul who is being led out of the Old Covenant bondage with its failure, into the real experience of the promise and power of the New Covenant.[6] In thus studying the work of the Mediator in an individual, we may get a truer conception of the real glory and greatness of the work He actually accomplishes than when we only think of the work He has done for all. It is in the application of the redemption here in the life of earth, where sin abounded, that its power is seen. Let us see how the entrance into the New Covenant blessing is attained.

---

[6] For a practical illustration in the life of Canon Battersby, see Note D.

The first step towards it in one who has been truly converted and assured of his acceptance with God is, the sense of sin. He sees that the New Covenant promises are not made true in his experience. There is not only indwelling sin, but he finds that he gives way to temper and self-will and worldliness, and other known transgressions of God's law. The obedience to which God calls and will fit him, the life of abiding in Christ's love which is his privilege, the power for a holy walk, well-pleasing to God,—in all this his conscience condemns him. It is in this conviction of sin that any thought or desire of the full New Covenant blessing must have its rise. Where the thought that obedience is an impossibility, and that nothing but a life of failure and self-condemnation is to be looked for, has wrought a secret despair of deliverance, or contentment with our present state, it is vain to speak of God's promise or power. The heart does not respond: it knows well enough, it is sure, the liberty spoken of is a dream. But where the dissatisfaction with our state has wrought a longing for something better, the heart is open to receive the message.

The New Covenant is meant to be the deliverance from the power of sin; a keen longing for this is the indispensable preparation for entering fully into the Covenant.

Now comes the second step. As the mind is directed to the literal meaning of the terms of the New Covenant, in its promises of cleansing from sin, and a heart filled with God's fear and God's law, and a power to keep God's commands and never to depart from Him; as the eye is fixed on Jesus the Surety of the Covenant, who will Himself make it all true; and as the voice is heard of witnesses who can declare how, after years of bondage, all this has been fulfilled in them—the longing begins to grow into a hope, and the inquiry is made, as to what is needed to enter this blessed life.

Then follows another step. The heart-searching question comes whether we are willing to give up every evil habit, all our own self-will, all that is of the spirit of the world, and surrender ourselves to be wholly and exclusively for Jesus. God cannot take so complete possession of a man, and bless him so wonderfully, and work in him so mightily, unless

He has him very completely, yea, wholly for Himself. Happy the man who is ready for any sacrifice.

Now comes the last, the simplest, and yet often the most difficult step. And here it is we need to know Jesus as Mediator of the Covenant. As we hear of the life of holiness and obedience and victory over sin which the Covenant promises, and hear that it will be to us according to our faith, so that if we claim it in faith it will surely be ours, the heart often fails for fear. I am willing, but have I the power to make, and what is more, to maintain this full surrender? Have I the power, the strong faith, so to grasp and hold this offered blessing that it shall indeed be and continue mine? How such questions perplex the soul until it finds the answer to them in the one word: Jesus! *It is He who will bestow the power to make the surrender and to believe.* This is as surely and as exclusively His work, as atonement and intercession are His alone. As sure as it was His to win and ascend the throne, it is His to prove His dominion in the individual soul. It is He, the Living One, who is in Divine power to work and maintain the life of communion and victory within us. He is the Mediator and Surety of the Covenant—He, the God-man, who has undertaken not only for all that God requires, but for all that we need too.

When this is seen, the believer learns that here, just as at conversion, it is all of faith. The one thing needed now is, with the eye definitely fixed on some promise of the New Covenant, to turn from self and anything it could or need do, to let go self, and fall into the arms of Jesus. He is the Mediator of the New Covenant: it is His to lead us into it. In the assurance that Jesus, and every New Covenant blessing, is already ours in virtue of our being God's children; with the desire now to appropriate and enjoy what we have hitherto allowed to lie unused; in the faith that Jesus now gives us the needed strength in faith to claim and accept our heritage as a present possession; the will dares boldly to do the deed, and to take the heavenly gift—a life in Christ according to the better promises. By faith in Jesus you have seen and received Him as to you, in full truth, the Mediator of the New Covenant, both in heaven

57

and in your heart. He is the Mediator who makes it true between God *and you,* as your experience.

The fear has sometimes been expressed that, if we press so urgently the work that Christ through the Spirit does in the heart, we may be drawn off from trusting in what He has done and ever is doing, to what we are experiencing of its working. The answer is simple. It is *with the heart alone* that Christ can be truly known or honoured. It is *in the heart* the work of grace is to be done, and the saving power of Christ to be displayed. It is *in the heart* alone the Holy Spirit has His sphere of work; *there* He is to work Christ's likeness; it is *there* alone He can glorify Christ. The Spirit can only glorify Christ by revealing His saving power *in us.* If we were to speak of what *we are to do* in cleansing our heart and keeping it right, the fear would be well-grounded. But the New Covenant calls us to the very opposite. What it tells us of the Atonement, and the righteousness of God it has won for us, will be our only glory even amid the highest holiness of heaven: Christ's work of holiness here in the heart can only deepen the consciousness of that righteousness as our only plea. The sanctification of the Spirit, as the fulfilment of the New Covenant promises, is all a taking of the things of Christ and revealing and imparting it to us. The deeper our entrance into and our possession of the New Covenant gift of a new heart, the fuller will be our knowledge and our love of Him who is its Mediator; the more we shall glory in Him alone. The Covenant deals with the heart, just that Christ may be found there, may *dwell there by faith.* As we look at the heart, not in the light of feeling or experience, but in the light of the faith of God's Covenant, we shall learn to think and speak of it as God does, and begin to know what it is, that there Christ manifests Himself and there He and the Father come to make their abode.

11

Jesus, the Surety of the Better Covenant

"And inasmuch as it is not without the taking of an oath: by so much also hath Jesus become the Surety of a better covenant. Wherefore also He is able to save completely them that draw near unto God through Him, seeing He ever liveth to make intercession for them" (Hebrews 7:20, 22, 25).

A SURETY IS ONE WHO stands good for another, that a certain engagement will be faithfully performed. Jesus is the Surety of the New Covenant. He stands surety with us for God—that God's part in the Covenant will faithfully be performed. And He stands surety with God for us, that our part will be faithfully performed too. If we are to live in covenant with God, everything depends upon our knowing aright what Jesus secures to us. The more we know and trust Him, the more assured will our faith be that its every promise and every demand will be fulfilled, that a life of faithful keeping of God's Covenant is indeed possible, because Jesus is the Surety of the Covenant. He makes God's faithfulness and ours equally sure.

We read that it was because His priesthood was confirmed by the oath of God, that He became the Surety of a so much better Covenant. The oath of God gives us the security that His suretyship will secure all the better promises. The meaning and infinite value of God's oath had been explained in the previous chapter.

"In every dispute the oath is final for confirmation. Wherein God, being minded to show more abundantly unto the heirs of the promise the immutability of His counsel, interposed with an oath, that by two immutable things, in which it is impossible for God to lie, we may have a strong encouragement."

We thus have not only a Covenant, with certain definite promises; we have not only Jesus the Surety of the Covenant; but at the back of that again, we have the living God, with a view to our having perfect

59

confidence in the unchangeableness of His counsel and promise, coming in between with an oath. Do we not begin to see that the one thing God aims at in this Covenant, and asks with regard to it, is an absolute confidence that He is going to do all He has promised, however difficult or wonderful it may appear? His oath is an end of all fear or doubt. Let no one think of understanding the Covenant, of judging or saying what may be expected from it, much less of experiencing its blessings, until he meets God with an Abraham-like faith, that gives Him the glory, and is fully assured that what He has promised He is able to perform. The Covenant is a sealed mystery, except to the soul who is going without reserve to trust God, and abandon itself to His word and work.

Of the work of Christ, as the Surety of the better Covenant, our passage tells us that, because of this priesthood confirmed by oath, He is able to save completely those who draw near to God through Him. And this, because "He ever liveth to make intercession for them." As Surety of the Covenant, He is ceaselessly engaged in watching their needs, and presenting them to the Father, in receiving His answer, and imparting its blessing. It is because of this never-ceasing mediation, receiving and transmitting from God to us the gifts and powers of the heavenly world, that He is able to save completely—to work and maintain in us a salvation as complete as God is willing it should be, as complete as the Better Covenant has assured us it shall be in the better promises upon which it was established. These promises are expounded (8:7-13) as being none other than those of the New Covenant of Jeremiah, with the law written in the heart by the Spirit of God as our experience of the power of that salvation.

Jesus, the Surety of a better Covenant, Jesus is to be our assurance that everything connected with the Covenant is unchangeably and eternally sure. In Jesus the keynote is given of all our intercourse with God, of all our prayers and desires, of all our life and walk, that with full assurance of faith and hope we may look for every word of the Covenant to be made fully true to us by God's own power. Let us look at some of these things of which we are to be fully assured, if we are to breathe the spirit of children of the New Covenant.

There is the love of God. The very thought of a Covenant is an alliance of friendship. And it is as a means of assuring us of His love, of drawing us close to His heart of love, of getting our hearts under the power of His love, and filled with it—it is because God loves us with an infinite love, and wants us to know it, and to give it complete liberty to bestow itself on us, and bless us, that the New Covenant has been made, and God's own Son been made its Surety. This love of God is an infinite Divine energy, doing its utmost to fill the soul with itself and its blessedness. Of this love God's Son is the Messenger; of the Covenant in which God reveals it to us He is the Surety; let us learn that the chief need in studying the Covenant and keeping it, in seeking and claiming its blessings, is the exercise of a strong and confident assurance in God's love.

Then there is the assurance of the sufficiency of Christ's finished redemption. All that was needed to put away sin, to free us entirely and for ever from its power, has been accomplished by Christ. His blood and death, His resurrection and ascension, have taken us out of the power of the world and transplanted us into a new life in the power of the heavenly world. All this is Divine reality; Christ is Surety that the Divine righteousness, and the Divine acceptance, that all-sufficient Divine grace and strength, are ever ours. He is Surety that all these can and will be communicated to us in unbroken continuance.

It is even so with the assurance of what is needed on our part to enter into this life in the New Covenant: we shrink back, either from the surrender of all, because we know not whether we have the power to let it go, or from the faith, because we fear ours will never be so strong or so bold as to take and hold all that is offered us in this wonderful Covenant. Jesus is Surety of a better Covenant. The better consists just in this very thing, that it undertakes to provide the children of the Covenant with the very dispositions they need, to accept and enjoy it. We have seen how the heart is just the central object of the Covenant promise. A heart circumcised to love God with all the heart, a heart into which God's law and fear have been put, so that it will not depart from Him—it is of all this Jesus is the Surety under the oath of God. Let us say it once more: Surely the one thing God asks of us, and has given the Covenant and its Surety to secure—*the confident trust that all will be done in us that is needed*—is what we dare not withhold.

I think some of us are beginning to see what has been our great mistake. We have thought and spoken great things of what Christ did on the Cross, and does on the Throne, as Covenant Surety. And we have stopped there. *But we have not expected Him to do great things in our hearts.* And yet it is there, in our heart, that the consummation takes place of the work on the Cross and the Throne; in the heart the New Covenant has its full triumph; the Surety is to be known not by what the mind can think of Him in heaven, but by what he does to make Himself known in the heart. *There* is the place where His love triumphs and is enthroned. Let us with the heart believe and receive Him as the Covenant Surety. Let us, with every desire we entertain in connection with it, with every duty it calls us to, with every promise it holds out, look to Jesus, under God's oath the Surety of the Covenant. Let us believe that by the Holy Spirit the heart is His home and His throne. Let us, if we have not done it yet, in a definite act of faith, throw ourselves utterly on Him, for the whole of the New Covenant life and walk. No surety was ever so faithful to his undertaking *as Jesus will be to His on our behalf, in our hearts.*

And now, notwithstanding the strong confidence and consolation the oath of God and the Surety of the Covenant gives, there are some still looking wistfully at this blessed life, and yet afraid to trust themselves to this wondrous grace. They have a conception of faith as something great and mighty, and they know and feel that theirs is not such. And so their feebleness remains an insuperable barrier to their inheriting the promise. Let me try and say once again: Brother, the act of faith, by which you accept and enter this life in the New Covenant, is not commonly an act of power, but often of weakness and fear and much trembling. And even in the midst of all this feebleness, it is not an act in your strength, but in a secret and perhaps unfelt strength, which Jesus the Surety of the Covenant gives you. God has made Him Surety, with the very object of inspiring us with courage and confidence. He longs, He delights to bring you into the Covenant. Why not bow before

Him, and say meekly: He does hear prayer; He brings into the Covenant; He enables a soul to believe; I may trust Him confidently. And just begin quietly to believe that there is an Almighty Lord, given by the Father, to do everything needed to make *all* Covenant grace wholly true in you. Bow low, and look up out of your low estate to your glorified Lord, and maintain your confidence that a soul, that in its nothingness trusts in Him, will receive more than it can ask or think.

Dear believer, come and be a believer. Believe that God is showing you how entirely the Lord Jesus wants to have you and your life for Himself; how entirely He is willing to take charge of you and work all in you; how entirely you may even now commit your trust, and your surrender, and your faithfulness to the Covenant, with all you are and are to be, to Him, your Blessed Surety. If thou believest, thou shalt see the glory of God.

In a sense, and measure, and power that passeth knowledge, Jesus Christ is Himself all that God can either ask or give, all that God wants to see in us. *"He that believeth in Me,* out of him shall flow rivers of living water."

12
The Book of the Covenant

"And Moses took the book of the covenant, and read in the audience of the people: and they said, All that the Lord hath said will we do and be obedient. And Moses took the blood, and sprinkled it on the people, and said, Behold the blood of the covenant, which the Lord hath made with you concerning all these words" (Exodus 24:7, 8; comp. Hebrews 9:18-20).

HERE IS A NEW ASPECT in which to regard God's blessed Book. Before Moses sprinkled the blood, he read the Book of the Covenant, and obtained the people's acceptance of it. And when he had sprinkled it, he said, "Behold the blood of the covenant, which the Lord hath made *concerning all these words.*" The Book contained all the conditions of the Covenant; only through the Book could they know all that God asked of them, and all that they might ask of Him. Let us consider what new light may be thrown both upon the Covenant and upon the Book, by the one thought that the Bible is the Book of the Covenant.

The very first thought suggested will be this, that in nothing will the spirit of our life and experience, as it lives either in the Old or the New Covenant, be more manifest than in our dealings with the Book. The Old had a book as well as the New. Our Bible contains both. The New was enfolded in the Old; the Old is unfolded in the New. It is possible to read the Old in the spirit of the New; it is possible to read the New as well as the Old in the spirit of the Old.

What this spirit of the Old is, we cannot see so clearly anywhere as just in Israel when the Covenant was made. They were at once ready to promise: "All that the Lord hath said will we do and be obedient." There was so little sense of their own sinfulness, or of the holiness and glory of God, that with perfect self-confidence they considered themselves able to undertake to keep the Covenant. They understood little of the meaning of that blood with which they were sprinkled, or of that death and redemption of which it was the symbol. In their own strength, in the power of the flesh, they were ready to undertake to serve God. It is just the spirit in which many Christians regard the Bible. It is a system of laws, a course of instruction to direct us in the way God would have us go. All He asks of us is, that we should do our utmost in seeking to fulfil them; more we cannot do; this we are sincerely ready to do. They know little or nothing of what the death means through which the Covenant is established, or what the life from the dead is through which alone a man can walk in covenant with the God of heaven.

This self-confident spirit in Israel is explained by what had happened just previously. When God had come down on Mount Sinai in thunderings and lightnings to give the law, they were greatly afraid. They said to Moses: "Let not God speak with us, lest we die; speak thou with us, and we will hear." They thought it was simply a matter of hearing and knowing; they could for certain obey. They knew not that it is only the presence, and the fear, and the nearness, and the power of God humbling us and making us afraid, that can conquer the power of sin and give the power to obey. It is so much easier to receive the instruction from man, and live, than to wait and hear the voice of God, and die to all our own strength and goodness. It is no otherwise that many Christians seek to serve God without ever seeking to live in daily contact with Him, and without the faith that it is only His presence can keep from sin. Their religion is a matter of outward instruction from man: the waiting to hear God's voice that they may obey Him, the death to the flesh and the world that comes with a close walk with God, are unknown. They may be faithful and diligent in the study of their Bible, in reading or hearing Bible teaching; to have as much as possible of that intercourse with the Covenant God Himself which makes the Christian life possible—this they do not seek.

If you would be delivered from all this, learn ever to read the Book of the New Covenant in the New Covenant Spirit. One of the very first articles of the New Covenant has reference to this matter. When God says, I will put My law in their inward parts, and write it in their hearts, He engages that the words of His Holy Book shall no longer be mere outward teaching, but that what they command shall be our very disposition and delight, wrought in us as a birth and a life by the Holy Spirit. Every word of the New Covenant then becomes a Divine assurance of what may be obtained by the Holy Spirit's working. The soul learns to see that the letter killeth, that the flesh profiteth nothing. The study, and knowledge of, the delight in, Bible words and thoughts, cannot profit, except as the Holy Spirit is waited on to make them life. The acceptance of Holy Scripture in the letter, in the human understanding and reception of it, is seen to be as fruitless as was Israel's at Sinai. But as the Word of God, spoken by the Living God through the Spirit into the heart that waits on Him, it is found to be quick and powerful. It then is a word that worketh effectually in them that believe, giving within the heart the actual possession of the very grace of which the Word has spoken.

The New Covenant is a ministration of the Spirit (see Chap. VII.). All its teaching is meant to be teaching by the Holy Spirit. The two most remarkable chapters in the Bible on the preaching of the gospel are those in which Paul expounds the secret of his teaching (1 Cor. 2; 2 Cor. 3). Every minister ought to see whether he can pass his examination in them. They tell us that in the New Covenant the Holy Spirit is everything. It was the Holy Spirit entering the heart, writing, revealing, impressing upon it God's law and truth, that could work true obedience. No excellency of speech or human wisdom can in the least profit: God must reveal by His Holy Spirit to preacher and hearer the things He hath prepared for us. What is true of the preacher is equally true of the hearer. One of the great reasons that so many Christians never come out of the Old Covenant, never even know that they are in it, and have to come out of it, is that there is so much head knowledge, without the power of the Spirit in the heart being waited for. It is only when preachers and hearers and readers believe that the Book of the New Covenant needs the Spirit of the New Covenant, to explain and apply it, that the Word of God can do its work.

Learn the double lesson. What God hath joined together, let no man put asunder. The Bible is the Book of the New Covenant. And the

Holy Spirit is the only minister of what belongs to the Covenant. Expect not to understand or profit by thy Bible knowledge without seeking continually the teaching of the Holy Spirit. Beware lest thy earnest Bible study, thy excellent books, or thy beloved teachers *take the place of the Holy Spirit!* Pray daily, and perseveringly, and believingly for His teaching. He will write the Word in thy heart.

The Bible is the Book of the New Covenant. Ask the Holy Spirit specially to reveal to thee the New Covenant in it. It is inconceivable what loss the Church of our day is suffering because so few believers truly live as its heirs, in the true knowledge and enjoyment of its promises. Ask God, in humble faith, to give thee in all thy Bible reading, the spirit of wisdom and revelation, enlightened eyes of thine heart, to know what the promises are which the Covenant reveals; and what the Divine security in Jesus, the Surety of the Covenant, that every promise will be fulfilled in thee in Divine power; and what the intimate fellowship to which it admits thee with the God of the Covenant. The ministration of the Spirit, humbly waited for and listened to, will make the Book of the Covenant shine with new light—even the light of God's countenance and a full salvation.

All this applies specially to the knowledge of what actually the New Covenant is meant to work. Amid all we hear, and read, and understand of the different promises of the New Covenant, it is quite possible that we never yet have had that heavenly vision of it as a whole, that with its overmastering power compels acceptance. Just hear once again what it really is. *The obedience, and fellowship with God,* for which man was created, which sin broke off, which the law demanded, but could not work, which God's own Son came from heaven to restore in our lives, *is now brought within our reach and offered us.* Our Father tells us in the Book of the New Covenant that He now expects us to live in full and unbroken obedience and communion with Him. He tells us that by the mighty power of His Son and Spirit *He Himself will work this in us:* everything has been arranged for it. He tells us that such a life of unbroken obedience is possible because Christ, as the Mediator, will live in us and enable us each moment to live in Him. He tells us that all He wants is simply the surrender of faith, the yielding ourselves to Him to do His work. Oh! let us look, and see *this holy life, with all its powers and blessings, coming down from God in heaven, in the Son and His Spirit.* Let us believe that the Holy Spirit can give us a vision of it, as a prepared Gift, to be bestowed in living power, and take possession of us. Let us look upward and look inward, in the faith of the Son and the Spirit, and God will show us that every word written in the Book of the Covenant is not only true, but that it can be made spirit and truth within us, and in our daily life. *This can indeed be.*

13
New Covenant Obedience

"Now therefore, *if ye will obey* My voice indeed, and keep My covenant, then ye shall be a holy nation unto Me" (Exodus 19:5).

"And the Lord Thy God will circumcise thine heart, and the heart of thy seed, *to hue the Lord thy God with all thy heart,* and with all thy soul. And *thou shalt obey* the voice of the Lord, and do all His commandments" (Deuteronomy 30:6, 8).

"And I will put My Spirit within you, and cause you to walk in My statutes, and *ye shall keep* My judgments" (Ezekiel 36:27).

IN MAKING THE NEW COVENANT, God said very definitely, "Not after the covenant I made with your fathers." We have learnt what the fault was with that Covenant: it made God's favour dependent upon the obedience of the people. *"If ye obey,* I will be your God." We have learnt how the New Covenant remedied the defect: God Himself provided for the obedience. It changes *"If ye keep* My judgments" into "I will put My Spirit within you, and *ye shall keep."* Instead of the Covenant and its fulfilment depending on man's obedience, God undertakes to ensure the obedience. The Old Covenant proved the need, and pointed out the path, of holiness: the New inspires the love, and gives the power, of holiness.

In connection with this change, a serious and most dangerous mistake is often made. Because in the New Covenant obedience no longer occupies the place it had in the Old, as the condition of the Covenant, and free grace has taken its place, justifying the ungodly, and bestowing gifts on the rebellious, many are under the impression that obedience is now *no longer as indispensable as it was then.* The error is a terrible one. The whole Old Covenant was meant to teach the lesson of the absolute and indispensable necessity of obedience for a life in God's favour. The New Covenant comes, not to provide a substitute for that obedience in faith, but through faith to secure the obedience, by giving a heart that delights in it and has the power for it. And men abuse the free grace, that without our own obedience accepts us for a life of new obedience, when they rest content with the grace, without the obedience it is meant for. They boast of the higher privileges of the New Covenant, while its chief blessing, *the power of a holy life, a heart delighting in God's law,* and a life in which God causes and enables us, by his indwelling Spirit, to keep His commandments, is neglected. If there is one thing we need to know well, it is the place obedience takes in the New Covenant.

Let our first thought be: *Obedience is essential.* At the very root of the relation of a creature to his God, and of God admitting the creature to His fellowship, lies the thought of obedience. It is the one only thing God spoke of in Paradise when "the Lord God commanded the man" not to eat of the forbidden fruit. In Christ's great salvation it is the power that redeemed us: "By the obedience of one shall many be made righteous." In the promise of the New Covenant it takes the first place. God engages to circumcise the hearts of His people—in the putting off of the body of the flesh, in the circumcision of Christ—to love God with all their heart, and to obey His commandments. The crowning gift of Christ's exaltation was the Holy Ghost, to bring salvation to us as an inward thing. The first Covenant demanded obedience, and failed because it could not find it. *The New Covenant was expressly made to provide for obedience.* To a life in the full enjoyment of the New Covenant blessing, obedience is essential.

It is this indispensable necessity of obedience that explains why so often the entrance into the full enjoyment of the New Covenant has depended upon some single act of surrender. There was something in the life, some evil or doubtful habit, in regard to which conscience had often said that it was not in perfect accord with God's perfect will. Attempts were made to push aside the troublesome suggestion. Or unbelief said it would be impossible to overcome the habit, and maintain the promise of obedience to the Voice within. Meantime, all our prayer appeared of no avail. It was as if faith could not lay hold of the blessing which was full in sight, until at last the soul consented to regard this little thing as the test of its surrender to obey in everything, and of its faith that in everything the Surety of the Covenant would give power to maintain the obedience. With the evil or doubtful thing given up, with a good conscience restored, and the heart's confidence before God assured, the soul could receive and possess what it sought. Obedience is essential.

Obedience is possible. The thought of a demand which man cannot possibly render, cuts at the very root of true hope and strength. The secret thought, "No man can obey God," throws thousands back into the Old Covenant life, and into a false peace that God does not expect more than that we do our best. Obedience is possible: the whole New Covenant promises and secures this.

Only understand aright what obedience means. The renewed man has still the flesh, with its evil nature, out of which there arise involuntary evil thoughts and dispositions. These may be found in a truly obedient man. Obedience deals with the doing of what is known to be God's will, as taught by the Word, and the Holy Spirit, and conscience. When George Müller spoke of the great happiness he had had for more than sixty years in God's service, he attributed it two things—He had loved God's Word, and "he had maintained a good conscience, not wilfully going on in a course he knew to be contrary to the mind of God." When the full light of God broke in upon Gerhard Tersteegen, he wrote: "I promise, with Thy help and power, rather to give up the last drop of my blood, than knowingly and willingly in my heart or my life be untrue and disobedient to Thee." Such obedience is an attainable degree of grace.

Obedience is possible. When the law is written in the heart; when the heart is circumcised to love the Lord with all our heart, and to obey Him; when the love of God is shed abroad in the heart; it means that the love of God's law and of Himself has now become the moving power of our life. This love is no vague sentiment, in man's imagination of something that exists in heaven, but a living, mighty power of God in the heart, working effectually according to His working, which worketh in us mightily. A life of obedience is possible.

This obedience is of faith. "By faith Abraham obeyed." By faith the promises of the Covenant, the presence of the Surety of the Covenant, the hidden in-working of the Holy Spirit, and the love of God in His infinite desire and power to make true in us all His love and promises, must live in us. Faith can bring them nigh, and make us live in the very midst of them. Christ and His wonderful redemption need not remain at a distance from us in heaven, but can become our continual experience. However cold or feeble we may feel, faith knows that the new heart is in us, that the love of God's law is our very nature, that the teaching and power of the Spirit are within us. Such faith knows it can obey. Let us hear the voice of our Saviour, the Surety of the Covenant, as He says, with a deeper, fuller meaning than when He was on earth: "Only believe. If thou canst believe, all things are possible to him that believeth."

And last of all, let us understand: *Obedience is a joy and a delight.* Do not regard it only as *the way* to the joy and blessings of the New Covenant, but as itself, in its very nature, part of that blessedness. To have the voice of God teaching and guiding you, to be united to God in willing what He wills, in working out what He works in you by His Spirit, in doing His Holy Will, and pleasing Him,—surely all this is joy unspeakable and full of glory.

To a healthy man it is a delight to walk or work, to put forth his strength and conquer difficulties. To a slave or a hireling it is bondage and weariness. The Old Covenant demanded obedience with an inexorable *must,* and the threat that followed it. The New Covenant changes the must to *can* and *may.* Do ask God, by the Holy Spirit, to show you how "you have been created in Christ Jesus unto good works," and how, as fitted as a vine is for bearing grapes, your new nature is perfectly prepared for every good work. Ask Him to show you that He means obedience, not only to be a possible thing, but the most delightful and attractive gift He has to bestow, the entrance into His love and all its blessedness.

In the New Covenant the chief thing is not the wonderful treasure of strength and grace it contains, nor the Divine security that that treasure never can fail, but this, that the living God gives Himself, and makes Himself known, and takes possession of us as our God. For this man was created, for this He was redeemed again, for this, that it may be our actual experience, the Holy Spirit has been given and is dwelling in us. Between what God has already wrought in us, and what He waits to work, obedience is the blessed link. Let us seek to walk before Him in the consciousness that we are of those who live in the noble and holy consciousness: my one work is to obey God.[7]

What can be the reason, I ask once again, that so many believers have seen so little of the beauty of this New Covenant life, with its power of holy and joyful obedience? "Their eyes were holden that they knew Him not." The Lord was with the disciples, but their hearts were blind. It is so still. It is as with Elisha's servant, all heaven is around him and he knows it not. Nothing will help but the prayer, "Lord, open his eyes, that he may see." Lord, is there not someone who may be reading this, who just needs one touch to see it all? Oh! give that touch!

Just listen, my brother. Thy Father loves thee with an infinite love, and longs to make thee, even to-day, His holy, happy, obedient child. Hear His message: He has for thee an entirely different life from what thou art living. *A life in which His grace shall actually work in thee every moment all He asks thee to be.* A life of simple childlike obedience, doing for the day just what the Father shows thee to be His will. A life in which the abiding love of thy Father, and the abiding presence of thy Saviour, and the joy of the Holy Spirit, can keep thee, and make thee glad and strong.

This is His message. This life is for thee. Fear not to accept this life, to give up thyself to it and its entire obedience. In Christ it is possible, it is sure.

Now, my brother, just turn heavenward and ask the Father, by the Holy Spirit, to show thee the beautiful heavenly life. Ask and expect it. Keep thine eyes fixed upon it. *The great blessing of the New Covenant is*

---

[7] In a volume just published, *The School of Obedience,* the thoughts of this chapter are more fully worked out.

obedience; the wonderful power to will and do as God wills. It is indeed the entrance to every other blessing. It is paradise restored and heaven opened the creature honouring his Creator, the Creator delighting in His creature; the child glorifying the Father, the Father glorifying the child, as He changes him, from glory to glory, into the likeness of His Son.

14

The New Covenant: A Covenant of Grace

"Sin shall not have dominion over you: for ye are not under the law, but under grace" (Romans 6:14).

THE WORDS, *Covenant of grace*, though not found in Scripture, are the correct expression of the truth it abundantly teaches, that the contrast between the two covenants is none other than that of law and grace. Of the New Covenant, grace is the great characteristic: "The law came in, that the offence might abound; but where sin abounded, grace did abound more exceedingly." It is to bring the Romans away entirely from under the Old Covenant, and to teach them their place in the New, that Paul writes: "Ye are not under the law, but under grace." And he assures them that if they believe this, and live in it, their experience would confirm God's promise: "Sin shall not have dominion over you." What the law could not do—give deliverance from the power of sin over us—grace would effect. The New Covenant was entirely a Covenant of grace. In the wonderful grace of God it had its origin; it was meant to be a manifestation of the riches and the glory of that grace; of grace, and by grace working in us, all its promises can be fulfilled and experienced.

The word *grace,* is used in two senses. It is first the gracious disposition in God *which moves Him* to love us freely without our merit, and to bestow all His blessings upon us. Then it also means that power which this grace bestows upon us to work in us. The redeeming work of Christ, and the righteousness He won for us, equally with the work of the Spirit in us, as the power of the new life, are spoken of as Grace. It includes all that Christ has done and still does, all He has and gives, all He is for us and in us. John says, "We beheld His glory, the glory of the Only Begotten of the Father, full of grace and truth." "The law was given by Moses; grace and truth came by Jesus Christ." "And of His

75

fulness have all we received, and grace for grace." What the law demands, grace supplies.

The contrast which John pointed out is expounded by Paul: "The law came in, that the offence might abound," and the way be prepared for the abounding of grace more exceedingly. The law points the way, but gives no strength to walk in it. The law demands, but makes no provision for its demands being met. The law burdens and condemns and slays. It can waken desire, but not satisfy it. It can rouse to effort, but not secure success. It can appeal to motives, but gives no inward power beyond what man himself has. And so, while warring against sin, it became its very ally in giving the sinner over to a hopeless condemnation. "The strength of sin is the law."

To deliver us from the bondage and the dominion of sin, grace came by Jesus Christ. Its work is twofold. Its exceeding abundance is seen in the free and full pardon there is of all transgression, in the bestowal of a perfect righteousness, and in the acceptance into God's favour and friendship. "In Him we have redemption through His blood, the forgiveness of sin according to the riches of His grace." It is not only at conversion and our admittance into God's favour, but throughout all our life, at each step of our way, and amid the highest attainments of the most advanced saint; we owe everything to grace, and grace alone. The thought of merit and work and worthiness is for ever excluded.

The exceeding abundance of grace is equally seen in the work which the Holy Spirit every moment maintains within us. We have found that the central blessing of the New Covenant, flowing from Christ's redemption and the pardon of our sins, is the new heart in which God's law and fear and love have been put. It is in the fulfilment of this promise, *in the maintenance of the heart in a state of meetness for God's indwelling,* that the glory of grace is specially seen. In the very nature of things this must be so. Paul writes: "Where sin abounded, grace did more exceedingly abound." And where, as far as I was concerned, did sin abound? All the sin in earth and hell could not harm me, were it not for its presence in my heart. It is there it has exercised its terrible dominion. And it is there the exceeding abundance of grace must be proved, if it is to benefit me. All grace in earth and heaven could not help me; it is only in the heart it can be received, and known, and enjoyed. "Where sin abounded," in the heart, there "grace did more exceedingly abound; that as sin reigned in death," working its destruction in the heart and life, "even so might grace reign," in the heart too, "through righteousness into eternal life, through Jesus Christ our Lord." As had been said just before, "They that receive the abundance of grace shall reign in life through Jesus Christ."

Of this reign of grace in the heart Scripture speaks wondrous things. Paul speaks of the grace that fitted him for his work, of "the gift of that grace of God which was given me according to the working of His power." "The grace of our Lord was exceeding abundant, with faith and love." "*The grace* which was bestowed upon me was not found vain, but *I laboured more abundantly* than they all; yet not I, but *the grace* of God which was with me." "He said unto me, *My grace* is sufficient for thee; My strength is made perfect in weakness." He speaks in the same way of grace as working in the life of believers, when he exhorts them to "be strong in the grace that is in Christ Jesus"; when he tells us of "the grace of God" exhibited in the liberality of the Macedonian Christians, and "the exceeding grace of God" in the Corinthians; when he encourages them: "God is able to make all grace abound in you, that ye may abound unto every good work." Grace is not only the power that moves the heart of God in its compassion towards us, when He acquits and accepts the sinner and makes him a child, but is equally the power that moves the heart of the saint, and provides it each moment with just the disposition and the power which it needs to love God and do His will.

It is impossible to speak too strongly of the need there is to know that, as wonderful and free and alone sufficient as is the grace that pardons, is the grace that sanctifies; we are just as absolutely dependent upon the latter as the former. We can do as little to the one as the other. The grace that works in us must as exclusively do all in us and through us as the grace that pardons does all for us. In the one case as the other, everything is by faith alone. Not to apprehend this brings a double danger. On the one hand, people think that grace cannot be more exalted than in the bestowal of pardon on the vile and unworthy; and a secret feeling arises that, if God be so magnified by our sins more than anything else, we must not expect to be freed from them in this life. With many this cuts at the root of the life of true holiness. On the other hand, from not knowing that grace is always and alone to do all the work in our sanctification and fruit-bearing, men are thrown upon their own efforts, their life remains one of feebleness and bondage under the law, and they never yield themselves to let grace do all it would.

Let us listen to what God's Word says: *"By grace* have ye been saved, *through faith;* not of works, lest any man should glory. For we are His workmanship, created in Christ Jesus for good works, which God afore prepared that we should walk in them." Grace stands in contrast to good works of our own not only before conversion, but after conversion too. We are created *in Christ Jesus* for good works, which God had prepared for us. It is grace alone can work them in us and work them out through us. Not only the commencement but the continuance of the Christian life is the work of grace. "Now if it is by grace it is no more of works, otherwise grace is no more grace; therefore it is of faith that it may be according to grace." As we see that grace is literally and absolutely to do all in us, so that all our actings are the showing forth of grace in us, we shall consent to live the life of faith—a life in which, every moment, everything is expected from God. It is only then that we shall experience that sin shall not, never, not for a moment, have dominion over us.

"Ye are not under the law, but under grace." There are three possible lives. One entirely under the law; one entirely under grace; one a mixed life, partly law, partly grace. It is this last against which Paul warns the Romans. It is this which is so common, and works such ruin among Christians. Let us find out whether this is not our position, and the cause of our low state. Let us beseech God to open our eyes by the Holy Spirit to see that in the New Covenant everything, every movement, every moment of our Christian life, is of grace, abounding grace; grace abounding exceedingly, and working mightily. Let us believe that our Covenant God waits to cause all grace to abound toward us. And let us begin to live the life of faith that depends upon, and trusts in, and looks to, and ever waits for God, through Jesus Christ, by the Holy Spirit, to work in us that which is pleasing in His sight.

Grace unto you, and peace be multiplied!

15
The Covenant of an Everlasting Priesthood

"That My covenant might be with Levi. My covenant was with him of life and peace; and I gave them to him for the fear wherewith he feared Me, and was afraid before My name. The law of truth was in his mouth, and iniquity was not found in his lips; he walked with Me in peace and equity, and did turn many away from iniquity" (Malachi 2:4-6).

ISRAEL WAS MEANT by God to be a nation of priests. In the first making of the Covenant this was distinctly stipulated. "If ye will obey My voice, and keep My covenant, ye shall be unto Me a kingdom of priests." They were to be the stewards of the oracles of God; the channels through whom God's knowledge and blessing were to be communicated to the world; in them all nations were to be blessed.

Within the people of Israel one tribe was specially set apart to embody and emphasise the priestly idea. The first-born sons of the whole people were to have been the priests. But to secure a more complete separation from the rest of the people, and the entire giving up of any share in their possessions and pursuits, God chose one tribe to be exclusively devoted to the work of proving what constitutes the spirit and the power of priesthood. Just as the priesthood of the whole people was part of God's Covenant with them, so the special calling of Levi is spoken of as God's Covenant of Life and Peace being with Him, as the Covenant of an everlasting priesthood. All this was to be a picture to help them and us, in some measure, to apprehend the priesthood of His own Blessed Son, the Mediator of the New Covenant.

Like Israel, all God's people, under the New Covenant, are a royal priesthood. The right of free and full access to God, the duty and power of mediating for our fellowmen and being God's channel of blessing to them, is the inalienable birthright of every believer. Owing to the feebleness and incapacity of many of God's children, their ignorance of the mighty grace of the New Covenant, they are utterly impotent to take up and exercise their priestly functions. To make up for this lack of service, to show forth the exceeding riches of His grace in the New Covenant, and the power He gives men of becoming, just as the priests of old were the forerunners of the Great High Priest, His followers and representatives, God still allows and invites those of His redeemed ones who are willing, to offer their lives to this blessed ministry. To him who accepts the call, the New Covenant brings in special measure what God has said: "My Covenant of Life and Peace shall be with him"; it becomes to him in very deed "the Covenant of an everlasting priesthood." As the Covenant of Levi's priesthood issued and culminated in Christ's, ours issues from that again, and receives from it its blessing to dispense to the world.

To those who desire to know the conditions on which, as part of the New Covenant, the Covenant of an everlasting priesthood can be received and carried out, a study of the conditions on which Levi received the priesthood will be most instructive. We are not only told that God chose that tribe, but what there specially was in that tribe that fitted it for the work. Malachi says: "I gave him My covenant for the fear wherewith he feared Me, and was afraid before My name." The reference is to what took place at Sinai when Israel had made the molten calf. Moses called all who were on the Lord's side, who were ready to avenge the dishonour done to God, to come to him. The tribe of Levi did so, and at his bidding took their swords, and slew three thousand of the idolatrous people (Ex. 32:26-29). In the blessing with which Moses blessed the tribes before his death, their absolute devotion to God, without considering relative or friend, is mentioned as the proof of their fitness for God's service (Deut. 33:8-11):

"Let Thy Thummim and Thy Urim be with Thy holy one, who said unto his father and to his mother, I have not known thee; neither did he acknowledge his own brethren, nor know his own children: for they have observed Thy word and kept Thy covenant."

The same principle is strikingly illustrated in the story of Aaron's grandson, Phineas, where he, in his zeal for God, executed judgment on disobedience to God's command. The words are most suggestive.

> "And the Lord spake unto Moses, saying, Phineas, the son of Eleazar, the son of Aaron, hath turned away My wrath from the children of Israel, in that *he was jealous with My jealousy* among them, so that I consumed them not in My jealousy. Wherefore say, Behold, I give unto him My covenant of peace: and it shall be unto him, and his seed after him, the covenant of an everlasting priesthood; because *he was jealous for his God,* and made an atonement for the children of Israel" (Num. 25:10-13).

To be jealous with God's jealousy, to be jealous for God's honour, and rise up against sin, is the gate into the Covenant of an everlasting priesthood, is the secret of being entrusted by God with the sacred work of teaching His people, and burning incense before Him, and turning many from iniquity (Deut. 33:10; Mal. 2:6).

Even the New Covenant is in danger of being abused by the seeking of our own happiness or holiness, more than the honour of God or the deliverance of men. Even where these are not entirely neglected, they do not always take the place they are meant to have—that first place that makes everything, the dearest and best, secondary and subordinate to the work of helping and blessing men. A reckless disregard of everything that would interfere with God's will and commands, a being jealous with God's jealousy against sin, a witnessing and a fighting against it at any sacrifice—this is the school of training for the priestly office.

It is this the world needs nowadays—men of God in whom the fire of God burns, men who can stand and speak and act in power on behalf of a God who, amid His own people, is dishonoured by the worship of the golden calf. Understand that as you will, of the place given to money and rich men in the church, of the prevalence of worldliness and luxury, or of the more subtle danger of a worship meant for the true God, under forms taken from the Egyptians, and suited to the wisdom and the carnal life of this world. A religion God cannot approve is often found even where the people still profess to be in covenant with God. "Consecrate yourselves to-day unto the Lord, even every man upon his brother." This call of Moses is as much needed to-day as ever. To each one who responds there is the reward of the priesthood.

Let all who would know to the full what the New Covenant means, remember God's Covenant of Life and Peace with Levi. Accept of the holy calling to be an intercessor, and to burn incense before the Lord continually. Live, work, pray, believe, as one God has sought and found to stand in the gap before Him. The New Covenant was dedicated by a sacrifice and a death: reckon it your most wonderful privilege, your fullest entrance into its life, as you reflect the glory of the Lord, and are changed into the same image from glory to glory, as by the Spirit of the Lord, to let the Spirit of that sacrifice and death be the moving power in all your priestly functions. Sacrifice yourself, live and die for your fellowmen.

One of the great objects with which God has made a Covenant with us, is, as we have said so often, to waken strong confidence in Himself and His faithfulness to His promise. And one of the objects that He has in wakening and so strengthening the faith in us, is that He may use us as His channels of blessing to the world. In the work of saving men, He wants intercessory prayer to take the first place. He would have us come to Him to receive, from Him in heaven, the spiritual life and power which can pass out from us to them. He knows how difficult and hopeless it is in many cases to deal with sinners; He knows that it is no light thing for us to believe that in answer to our prayer the mighty power of God will move to save those around us; He knows that it needs strong faith to persevere patiently in prayer in cases in which the answer is long delayed, and every year appears farther off than ever. And so He undertakes, in our own experience, to prove what faith in His Divine power can do, in bringing down all the blessings of the New Covenant on ourselves, that we may be able to expect confidently what we ask for others.

In our priestly life there is still another aspect. The priests had no inheritance with their brethren; the Lord God was their inheritance.

They had access to His dwelling and His presence, that there they might intercede for others, and thence testify of what God is and wills. Their personal privilege and experience fitted them for their work. If we would intercede in power, do let us live in the full realisation of New Covenant life. It gives us not only liberty and confidence with God, and power to persevere; it gives us power with men, as we can testify to and prove what God has done to us. Herein is the full glory of the New Covenant, that, like Christ, its

Mediator, we have the fire of the Divine love dwelling in us, and consuming us in the service of men. May to each of us the chief glory of the New Covenant be that it is the Covenant of an everlasting priesthood.

16
The Ministry of the New Covenant

"Ye are our epistle, written in our hearts, known and read of all men: being made manifest that ye are an epistle of Christ, ministered by us, written not with ink, but with the Spirit of the living God: not in tables of stone, but in tables that are hearts of flesh. And such confidence have we through Christ Godward: not that we are sufficient of ourselves, to account anything as from ourselves; but our sufficiency is from God; who also made us sufficient as ministers of a new covenant; not of the letter, but of the Spirit; for the letter killeth, but the Spirit giveth life" (2 Corinthians 3:2-6).

WE HAVE SEEN THAT the New Covenant is a ministration of the Spirit. The Holy Spirit ministers all its grace and blessing in Divine power and life.[8] He does this through men, who are called ministers of a New Covenant, ministers of the Spirit. The Divine ministration of the Covenant to men, and the earthly ministry of God's servants, are equally to be in the power of the Holy Spirit. The ministry of the New Covenant has its glory and its fruit in this, that it is all to be a demonstration of the Spirit and of power.

What a contrast this to the Old Covenant. Moses had indeed received of the glory of God shining upon him, but had to put a veil on his face. Israel was incapable of looking on it. In hearing and reading Moses, there was a veil on their hearts. From Moses they might receive knowledge and thoughts and desires,—the power of God's Spirit, to enable them to see the glory of what God speaks, was not yet given. This is the exceeding glory of the New Covenant, that it is a ministration of the Spirit; that its ministers have their sufficiency from God, who makes them ministers of the Spirit, and makes them able so to speak the words of God in the Spirit, so that they are written in the heart, and that

---

[8] It may be well to read again and compare Chapter 7: "The New Covenant: A Ministration of the Spirit."

the hearers become legible, living epistles of Christ, showing the law written in their heart and life.

The ministry of the Spirit! What a glory there is in it! What a responsibility it brings! What a sufficiency of grace there is provided for it! What a privilege, to be a minister of the Spirit!

What tens of thousands we have throughout Christendom who are called ministers of the gospel. What an inconceivable influence they exert for life or for death over the millions who depend upon them for their knowledge and participation of the Christian life. What a power there would be if all these were ministers of the Spirit! Let us study the word, until we see what God meant the ministry to be, and learn to take our part in praying and labouring to have it nothing less.

God hath made us ministers of the Spirit. The first thought is that a minister of the New Covenant must be a man personally possessed of the Holy Spirit. There is a twofold work of the Spirit: one in giving a holy disposition and character, the other in qualifying and empowering a man for work. The former must always come first. The promise of Christ to His disciples, that they should receive the Holy Spirit for their service, was very definitely given to those who had followed and loved Him, and kept His commandments. It is by no means enough that a man have been born of the Spirit. If he is to be a "sufficient minister" of the New Covenant, he must know what it is to be led by the Spirit, to walk in the Spirit, and to say, "The law of the Spirit of life in Christ Jesus hath made me free from the law of sin and death." Who that wants to learn Greek or Hebrew would accept a professor who hardly knows the elements of these languages? And how can a man be a minister of the New Covenant, which is so entirely "a ministration of the Spirit," a ministration of heavenly life and power, unless he knows by experience what it is to live in the Spirit? The minister must, before everything, be a personal proof and witness of the truth and power of God in the fulfilment of what the New Covenant promises. Ministers are to be picked men; the best specimens and examples of what the Holy Spirit can do to sanctify a man, and by the working of God's power in him to fit him for His service.

God hath made us ministers of the Spirit. Next to this thought, of being personally possessed by the Spirit, comes the truth that all their work in the ministry can be done in the power of the Spirit. What an unspeakably precious assurance—Christ sends them to do a heavenly work, to do His work, to be the instruments in His hands, by which He works: He clothes them with a heavenly power. Their calling is "to preach the gospel with the Holy Ghost sent down from heaven." As far as feelings are concerned, they may have to say as Paid: "I was with you in weakness, and in fear, and in much trembling." That does not prevent their adding, nay rather, that may just be the secret of their being able to add: "My preaching was in demonstration of the Spirit and of power." If a man is to be a minister of the New Covenant, a messenger and a teacher of its true blessing, so as to lead God's children to live in it, nothing less will do than a full experience of its power in himself, as the Spirit ministers it. Whether in his feeding on God's word himself, or his seeking in it for God's message for his people, whether in secret or intercessory prayer, whether in private intercourse with souls or public teaching, he is to wait upon, to receive, to yield to the energising of the Holy Spirit, as the mighty power of God working with him. This is his sufficiency for the work. He may every day afresh claim and receive the anointing with fresh oil, the new inbreathing from Christ of His own Spirit and life.

God hath made us ministers of the Spirit. There is something still, of no less importance. The minister of the Spirit must especially see to it that *he lead men to the Holy Spirit.* Many will say, If he be led of the Spirit in teaching men, is not that enough? By no means. Men may become too dependent on him; men may take his Scripture teaching at second-hand, and, while there is power and blessing in his ministry, have reason to wonder that the results are not more definitely spiritual and permanent. The reason is simple. The New Covenant is: they shall no longer every man teach his brother, know the Lord, for all shall know Me, from the least even to the greatest. The Father wants every child, from the least, to *live in continual personal intercourse with Himself.* This cannot be, except as he is taught and helped to know and wait on the Holy Spirit. Bible study and prayer, faith and love and obedience, the whole daily walk must be taught as entirely dependent on the teaching and working of the indwelling Spirit.

The minister of the Spirit, very definitely and perseveringly, points away from himself to the Spirit. This is what John the Baptist did. He was filled with the Holy Spirit from his birth, but sent men away from himself to Christ, to be by Him baptized with the Spirit. Christ did the same. In His farewell discourse He called His to disciples to turn from His personal instruction to the inward teaching of the Holy Spirit, who should dwell in them, and guide them into the truth and power of all He had taught them.

There is nothing so needed in the Church to-day. All its feebleness and formalities and worldliness, the lack of holiness, of personal devotion to Christ, of enthusiasm for His cause and kingdom, is owing to one thing—the Holy Spirit is not known and honoured and yielded to, as the one only, as the one all-sufficient source of a holy life. The New Covenant is not known as a ministration of the Spirit in the heart of every believer. The one thing needful for the Church is—the Holy Spirit in His power dwelling and ruling in the lives of God's saints. And as one of the chief means to this there are needed ministers of the Spirit, themselves living in the enjoyment and power of this great gift, who persistently labour to bring their brethren into the possession of their birthright: the Holy Spirit in the heart, maintaining, in Divine power, an unceasing communion with the Son and with the Father. The ministration of the Spirit makes the ministry of the Spirit possible and effectual. And the ministry of the Spirit again makes the ministration of the Spirit an actual experimental reality in the life of the Church.

We know how dependent the Church is on its ministry. The converse is no less true. The ministers are dependent on the Church. They are its children; they breathe its atmosphere; they share its health or sickliness; they are dependent upon its fellowship and intercession. Let none of us think that all that the New Covenant calls us to is to see that we personally accept and rejoice in its blessings. No, indeed; God wants everyone who enters into it to know that its privileges are for all

His children, and to give himself to make this known. And there is no more effectual way of doing this than taking thought for the ministry of the Church. Compare the ministry around you with its pattern in God's word (see specially 1 Cor. 2; 2 Cor. 3). Join with others who know how the New Covenant is nothing, if it be not a ministration of the Spirit, and cry to God for a spiritual ministry. Ask the leading of God the Holy Ghost to teach you what can be done, what you can do, to have the ministry of your Church become a truly spiritual one. Human condemnation will do as little good as human approbation. It is as the supreme place of the Holy Spirit, as the representative and revealer of the Father and the Son, is made clear to us, that the one desire of our heart, and our continual prayer, will be, that God would so discover to all the ministers of His word their heavenly calling, that they may, above everything, seek this one thing,—to be sufficient ministers of the New Covenant, not of the letter, but of the Spirit.

17
His Holy Covenant

"To remember His Holy Covenant, to grant unto us that we, being delivered out of the hands of our enemies, should serve Him without fear, in holiness and righteousness before Him, all our days" (Luke 1:68-75).

WHEN ZACHARIAS WAS FILLED with the Holy Spirit and prophesied, he spoke of God's visiting and redeeming His people, as a remembering of His Holy Covenant. He speaks of what the blessings of that Covenant would be, not in words that had been used before, but in what is manifestly a Divine revelation to him by the Holy Spirit; and gathers up all the former promises in these words: "That we should serve Him without fear, *in holiness and righteousness before Him all the days of our life.*" Holiness in life and service is to be the great gift of the Covenant of God's Holiness. As we have seen before, the Old Covenant proclaimed and demanded holiness; the New provides it; holiness of heart and life is its great gift.

There is no attribute of God so difficult to define, so peculiarly a matter of Divine revelation, so mysterious, incomprehensible, and inconceivably glorious, as His Holiness. It is that by which He is specially worshipped in His majesty on the throne of heaven (Isa. 6:2; Rev. 4:8, 15:4). It unites His righteousness, that judges and condemns, with His love, that saves and blesses. As the Holy One He is a consuming fire (Isa. 10:17); as the Holy One He loves to dwell among His people (Isa. 12:6). As the Holy One He is at an infinite distance from us; as the Holy One He comes inconceivably near, and makes us one with, makes us like Himself. The one purpose of His holy Covenant is to make us holy as He is holy.

As the Holy One He says: "I am holy; be ye holy; I am the Lord which hallow you, which make you holy." The highest conceivable summit of blessedness is our being partakers of the Divine nature, of the Divine holiness.

This is the great blessing Christ, the Mediator of the New Covenant, brings. He has been made unto us "both righteousness and sanctification"—righteousness in order to, as a preparation for, sanctification[9] or holiness. He prayed to the Father: "Sanctify them; for their sakes I *sanctify* Myself, that they themselves may also be *sanctified* in truth." In Him we are sanctified, saints, holy ones (Rom. 1:7; 1 Cor. 1:2). We have put on the new man which after God is created in righteousness and holiness. Holiness is our very nature.

We are holy in Christ. As we believe it, as we receive it, as we yield ourselves to the truth, and draw nigh to God to have the holiness drawn forth and revealed in fellowship with Him, its fountain, we shall know how divinely true it is.

It is for this the Holy Spirit has been given in our hearts. He is the "Spirit of Holiness." His every working is in the power of holiness. Paul says: "God hath *chosen us unto salvation, in sanctification of the Spirit* and belief of the truth." As simple and entire as is our dependence on the word of truth, as the external means, must our confidence be in the hidden power for holiness which the working of the Spirit brings. The connection between God's electing purpose, and the work of the Spirit, with the word we obey, comes out with equal clearness in Peter: *"Elect, in sanctification of the Spirit,* unto obedience." The Holy Spirit is the Spirit of the life of Christ; as we know, and honour, and trust Him, we shall learn and also experience that, in the New Covenant, as the ministration of the Spirit, the sanctification, the holiness of the Holy Spirit is our covenant right. We shall be assured that, as God has promised, so He will work it in us, that we "should serve Him without fear, in righteousness and holiness before Him, all the days of our life." With a treasure of holiness in Christ, and the very Spirit of holiness in our hearts, we can live holy lives. That is if we believe Him "who worketh in us both to will and to work."

In the light of this Covenant promise, with the Blessed Son and the Holy Spirit to work it out in us, what new meaning is given to the

---

[9] Remember that the words sanctify, sanctity, saint are the same as make holy, holiness, holy one.

teaching of the New Testament. Take the first epistle St. Paul ever wrote. It was directed to men who had only a few months previously been turned from idols to serve the Living God, and to wait for His Son from heaven. The words he speaks in regard to the holiness they might aim at and expect, because God was going to work it in them, are so grand that many Christians pass them by, as practically unintelligible (1 Thess. 3:13): "The Lord make you to increase and abound in love, to the end *He may stablish your hearts unblamable in holiness* at the coming of our Lord Jesus with all His saints." That promises holiness, unblamable holiness, a heart unblamable in holiness, a heart stablished in all this by God Himself. Paul might indeed say of a word like this: "Who hath believed our report?" He had written of himself (2:10): "Ye know how *holily* and *righteously* and *unblamably* we behaved ourselves." He assures them that what God has done for him He will do for them—give them hearts unblameable in holiness. The Church believes so little in the mighty power of God, and the truth of His Holy Covenant, that the grace of such heart-holiness is hardly spoken of. The verse is often quoted in connection with "the coming of our Lord Jesus with His saints"; but its real point and glory,—that when He comes we may meet Him with *hearts stablished unblamable in holiness* by God Himself. All too little this is proclaimed or expected.

Or take another verse in the epistle (v. 21), also spoken to these young converts from heathenism, in reference to the coming of our Lord. Some think that to speak much of the coming of the Lord will make us holy. Alas! how little it has done so in many cases. It is the New Covenant Holiness, wrought by God Himself in us, believed in and waited for from Him, that can make our waiting differ from the carnal expectations of the Jews or the disciples. Listen—"THE GOD OF PEACE HIMSELF"—that is the keynote of the New Covenant—what you never can do God will work in you—"SANCTIFY YOU WHOLLY"; this you may ask and expect,—*"and may your spirit and soul and body be preserved entire,* UNBLAMABLE, *at the coming of our Lord Jesus Christ."* And now, as if to meet the doubt that will arise: *"Faithful is He that calleth you,* WHO WILL ALSO DO IT." Again, it is the secret of the New Covenant—what hath not entered into the heart of man—GOD WILL WORK in them that wait for Him. Until the Church awakes to see and believe that our holiness is to be the *immediate almighty working of the Three-One God in us*, and that our whole religion must be an unceasing dependence to receive it *direct from Himself*, these promises remain a sealed book.

Let us now return to the prophecy of the Holy Spirit by Zacharias, of God's remembering the Covenant of His Holiness, to make us holy, to stablish our hearts unblamable in holiness, that we should serve Him IN HOLINESS AND RIGHTEOUSNESS. Note how every word is significant.

To grant us. It is to be a gift from above. The promise given with the Covenant was: "I the Lord have spoken it; *I will perform it.*" We need to beseech God to show us what *He will do*; when our faith expects all from Him, the blessing will be found.

"That we, being delivered out of the hands of our enemies." He had just before said. *He hath raised up an horn of salvation for us; salvation from our enemies and the hand of all that hate us.* It is only a free people can serve a Holy God, or be holy. It is only as the teaching of Rom. 6—8 is experienced, and I know what it is that we are "freed from sin," and "freed from the law," and that "the Spirit of life in Christ Jesus hath made me free from the law of sin and death," that in the perfect liberty from every power that could hinder, I can expect God to do His mighty work in me.

Should serve Him. My servant does not serve me by spending all his time in getting himself ready for work, but in doing my work. The Holy Covenant sets us free, and endows us with Divine grace, that God may have us for His work,—the same work Christ began, and we now carry on.

Without fear. In child-like confidence and boldness before God. And before men too. A freedom from fear in every difficulty, because having learnt to know that God works all in us we can trust Him to work all for us and through us.

Before Him. With His continued unceasing presence all the day as the unceasing security of our obedience and our fearlessness, the never-failing secret of our being sanctified wholly.

All our days. Not only all the day for one day, but for every day, because Jesus is a High Priest in the power of an endless life, and the mighty operation of God as promised in the Covenant is as unchanging as is God Himself.

Is it not as if you begin to see that God's word does appear to mean more than you have ever conceived of or expected? It is well that it should be so. It is only when you begin to say, *Glory to Him* who is able to do *exceeding abundantly above all* we can ask or think, and expect God's almighty, supernatural, altogether immeasurable power and grace to work out the New Covenant life in you, and *to make you holy,* that you will really come to the place of helplessness and dependence where God can work.

I pray you, my Brother, do believe that God's word is true, and say with Zacharias,

> "Blessed be the Lord, the God of Israel, who hath visited His people, to remember His HOLY COVENANT, and to grant us, that we, being delivered from the hand of our enemies, should serve Him without fear, *in holiness and righteousness before Him, all our days.*"

18

Entering the Covenant: With All the Heart

"And they entered into the covenant to seek the Lord God of their fathers with *all their heart,* and all their soul" (2 Chronicles 15:12, see 24:31, and 2 Kings 23:3).

"The Lord thy God will circumcise thine heart, to love the Lord thy God with *all thine heart,* and with all thy soul" (Deuteronomy 30:6).

"And I *will give them an heart* to know Me, that I am the Lord; and they shall be My people, and I will be their God: for they shall turn to Me with *their whole heart*" (Jeremiah 24:7, see 29:13).

"I will make an everlasting covenant with them, that I will not turn away from them, to do them good; but I will put My fear *in their hearts,* that they shall not depart from Me. Tea, I will rejoice over them to do them good, *with My whole heart and My whole soul*" (Jeremiah 32:40).

IN THE DAYS OF ASA, Hezekiah, and Josiah, we read of Israel entering into "the Covenant" with their whole heart, "to perform the words of the Covenant which are written in the book." Of Asa's day, we read: "They sware unto the Lord; and all Judah rejoiced at the oath, for they had sworn *with their whole heart,* and sought Him *with their whole desire;* and He was found of them." Wholeheartedness is the secret of entering the Covenant, and God being found of us in it. Wholeheartedness is the secret of joy in religion—a full entrance into all the blessedness the Covenant brings. God rejoices over His people to do them good, *with His whole heart and His whole soul:* it needs, on our part, *our whole heart and our whole soul* to enter into and enjoy this joy of God in doing us good with His whole heart and His whole soul. With what measure we mete, it shall be measured unto us again.

If we have at all understood the teaching of God's word in regard to the New Covenant, we know what it reveals in regard to the two parties who meet in it. On God's side there is the promise to do for us and in us all that we need to serve and enjoy Him. He will rejoice in doing us good, with His whole heart. He will be our God, doing for us all that a God can do, giving Himself as God to be wholly ours. And on our side there is the prospect held out of our being able, in the power of what He engages to do, to "turn to Him with our whole heart," "to love Him with all our heart and all our strength." The first and great commandment, the only possible terms on which God can fully reveal Himself, or give Himself to His creature to enjoy, is, "Thou shalt love the Lord thy God with all thy heart." That law is unchangeable. The New Covenant comes and brings us the grace to obey, by lifting us into the love of God as the air we breathe, and calls upon us, in the faith of that grace, to rise and be of good courage, and with our whole heart to yield ourselves to the God of the Covenant, and the life in His service.

Wholeheartedness in the love and the service of God! How shall I speak of it? Of its imperative necessity? It is the one unalterable condition of true communion with God, of which nothing can supply the want. Of its infinite reasonableness? With such a God, a very Fountain of all that is loving and lovely, of all that is good and blessed, the All-glorious God: surely there cannot for a moment be a thought of anything else being His due, or of our consenting to offer Him anything less, than the love of the whole heart. Of its unspeakable blessedness? To love Him with the whole heart, this is the only possible way of receiving His great love into our heart and rejoicing in it—yielding oneself to that great love, and allowing God Himself, just as an earthly love enters into us and makes us glad, to give us the taste and the joy of the heavenliness of that love. Of its terrible lack? Yes, what shall I speak of this? Where find words to open the eyes and reach the heart, and show how almost universal is the lack of true wholeheartedness in the faith and love of God, in the seeking to love Him with the whole heart, in the giving up everything to possess Him, to please Him, to be wholly possessed of Him? And then of the blessed certainty of its attainableness? The Covenant has provided for it. The Triune God will work it by taking possession of the heart, and dwelling there. The Blessed Mediator of the Covenant undertakes for all we have to do. His constraining love shed abroad in our hearts by the Holy Spirit can bring it and maintain it. Yes, I ask how shall I speak of all this?

Have we not spoken enough of it already in this book? Do we not need something more than words and thoughts? Is not what we need rather this—quietly to turn to the Holy Spirit who dwells in us, and in the faith of the light and the strength our Lord gives through Him, accept and act out what God tells us of the God-given heart He has placed within us, the God-wrought wholeheartedness He works? Surely the new heart which has been given us to love God with, with God's Spirit in it, is wholly for God. Let our faith accept and rejoice in the wondrous gift, and not fear to say: I will love Thee, O Lord, with my whole heart. Just think for a moment of what it means that God has given us such a heart.

We know what God's giving means. *His giving depends on our taking.* He does not force upon us spiritual possessions. He promises, and gives, in such measure as desire and faith are ready to receive. He gives in Divine power; as faith trusts and yields itself to that power, the gift becomes consciously and experimentally our possession.

As spiritual gifts God's bestowings *are not recognised by sense or reason.* "Ear hath not heard, neither have entered into the heart of man, *the things which God hath prepared* for them that love Him. But God hath *revealed them unto us by His Spirit.* We have received the Spirit which is of God, that we might *know the things which are freely given us of God."* It is as you yield yourself to be led and taught by the Spirit, that your faith will be able, despite of all lack of feeling, to rejoice in the possession of the new heart, and all that is given with it.

Then, *this Divine giving is continuous.* I bestow a gift on a man; he takes it, and I never see him again. So God bestows temporal gifts on men, and they never think of Him. But spiritual gifts are only to be received and enjoyed in unceasing communication with God Himself. The new heart is not a power I have in myself, like the natural endowments of thinking or loving. No, it is only in unceasing dependence upon, in close contact with, God, that the heavenly gift of a new heart can be maintained uninjured, can day by day become stronger.

It is only in God's immediate presence, in unceasing direct dependence on Him, that spiritual endowments are preserved.

Then, further, *spiritual gifts can only be enjoyed by acting them out in faith*. None of the graces of the Christian life, like love, or meekness, or boldness, can be felt or known, much less strengthened, until we begin to exercise them.

We must not wait to feel them, or to feel the strength for them; we must, in the obedience of the faith that they are given us, and hidden within us, practise them. Whatever we read of the new heart, and of all God has given into it in the New Covenant, must be boldly believed and carried out into action.

All this is especially true of wholeheartedness, and loving God with all our heart. You may at first be very ignorant of all it implies. God has planted the new heart in the midst of the flesh, which, with its animating principle, SELF, has to be denied, to be kept crucified, and by the Holy Spirit to be mortified. God has placed you in the midst of a world, from which, with all that is of it and its spirit, you are to come out and be entirely separate. God has given you your work in His kingdom, for which He asks all your interest, and time, and strength. In all these three respects you need wholeheartedness, to enable you to make the sacrifices that may be required. If you take the ordinary standard of Christian life around you, you will find that wholeheartedness, intense devotion to God and His service, is hardly thought of. How to make the best of both worlds, innocently to enjoy as much as possible of this present life, is the ruling principle, and, as a natural consequence, the present world secures the larger share of interest. To please *self* is considered legitimate, and the Christ-like life of *not pleasing self* has little place. Wholeheartedness will lead you, and enable you too, to accept Christ's command and sell all for the pearl of great price. Though at first afraid of what it may involve, do not hesitate to speak the word frequently in the ear of your Father: *with my whole heart*. You may count on the Holy Spirit to open up its meaning, to show you to what service or what sacrifice God calls you in it, to increase its power, to reveal its blessedness, to make it the very spirit of your life of devotion to your Covenant God.

And now, who is ready to enter into this New and Everlasting Covenant with his whole heart? Let each of us do it.

Begin by asking God very humbly to give you by the Spirit, who dwells in you, the vision of the heavenly life, of wholehearted love and obedience as it has actually been prepared for you in Christ. It is an existing reality, a spiritual endowment out of the life of God which can come upon you. It is secured to you in the Covenant, and in Christ Jesus, its Surety. Ask earnestly, definitely, believingly, that God reveal this to you. Rest not till you know fully what your Father means you to be, and has provided for your most certainly being.

When you begin to see why the New Covenant was given, and what it promises, and how divinely certain its promises are, *offer yourself to God unreservedly to be taken up into it*. Offer, if He will take you in, to love Him with your whole heart, and to obey Him with all your strength. Hold not back, be not afraid. God has sworn to do you good *with His whole heart*: do say, do not hesitate to say, that into this Covenant, in which *He promises to cause you* to turn to Him, and to love Him with your whole heart, you now enter with your whole heart. If there be any fear, just ask again and believingly for a vision of the Covenant life. God swearing to do you good with *His whole heart*; God undertaking to make and enable you to love and obey Him with *your whole heart*: the vision of this life will make you bold to say: Into this Covenant of a wholehearted love in God and in me I do with my whole heart now enter.

Let us close and part with this one thought. A redeeming God, rejoicing with His whole heart and whole soul to do us good, and to work in us all that is well-pleasing in His sight: this is the one side. Such is the God of the Covenant. Gaze upon Him. Believe Him. Worship Him. Wait upon Him, until the fire begin to burn, and your heart be drawn out with all its might to love this God. Then the other side. A redeemed soul, rejoicing with all its heart and all its soul in the love of this God, entering into the covenant of wholehearted love, and venturing, ere it knows, to say to Him: With my whole heart I do love Thee, God, my exceeding joy. Such are the children of the Covenant.

Beloved reader! rest not till you have entered in, through the Gate Beautiful, though Christ the door, into this temple of the love, of the heart, of God.

Note A—*The Second Blessing*

IN THE LIFE OF THE BELIEVER there sometimes comes a crisis, as clearly marked as his conversion, in which he passes out of a life of continual feebleness and failure to one of strength, and victory, and abiding rest. The transition has been called the Second Blessing. Many have objected to the phrase, as being unscriptural, or as tending to make a rule for all, what was only a mode of experience in some. Others have used it as helping to express clearly in human words what ought to be taught to believers as a possible deliverance from the ordinary life of the Christian, to one of abiding fellowship with God, and entire devotion to His service. In introducing it into the title of this book, I have indicated my belief that, rightly understood, the words express a scriptural truth, and may be a help to believers in putting clearly before them what they may expect from God. Let me try and make clear how I think we ought to understand it.

I have connected the expression with the two Covenants. Why was it that God made two Covenants—not one, and not three? Because there were two parties concerned. In the First Covenant man was to prove what he could do, and what he was. In the Second, God would show what He would do. The former was the time of needed preparation; the latter, the time of Divine fulfilment. The same necessity as there was for this in the race, exists in the individual too. Conversion makes of a sinner a child of God, full of ignorance and weakness, without any conception of what the whole-hearted devotion is that God asks of him, or the full possession God is ready to take of him. In some cases the transition from the elementary stage is by a gradual growth and enlightenment. But experiences teaches, that in the great majority of cases this healthy growth is not found. To those who have never found the secret of a healthy growth, of victory over sin and perfect rest in God, and have possibly despaired of ever finding it, because all their efforts have been failures, it has often been a wonderful help to learn that it is possible by a single decisive step, bringing them into a right relationship to Christ, His Spirit, and His strength, to enter upon an entirely new life.

What is needed to help a man to take that step is very simple. He must see and confess the wrongness, the sin, of the life he is living, not in harmony with God's will. He must see and believe in the life which Scripture holds out, which Christ Jesus promises to work and maintain in him. As he sees that his failure has been owing to his striving in his own strength, and believes that our Lord Jesus will actually work all in him in Divine power, he takes courage, and dares surrender himself to Christ anew. Confessing and giving up all that is of self and sin, yielding himself wholly to Christ and His service, he believes and receives a new power to live his life by the faith of the Son of God. The change is in many cases as clear, as marked, as wonderful, as conversion. For lack of a better name, that of A Second Blessing came most naturally.

When once it is seen how greatly this change is needed in the life of most Christians, and how entirely it rests on faith in Christ and His power, as revealed in the Word, all doubt as to its scripturalness will be removed. And when once its truth is seen, we shall be surprised to find how, throughout Scripture, in history and teaching, we find what illustrates and confirms it.

Take the twofold passage of Israel through water, first out of Egypt, then into Canaan. The wilderness journey was the result of unbelief and disobedience, allowed by God to humble them, and prove them, and show what was in their heart. When this purpose had been accomplished, a second blessing led them through Jordan, as mightily into Canaan, as the first had brought them through the Red Sea out of Egypt.

Or take the Holy Place and the Holiest of All, as types of the life in the two covenants, and equally in the two stages of Christian experience. In the former, very real access to God and fellowship with Him, but always with a veil between. In the latter, the full access into the immediate presence of God, and the full experience of the power of the heavenly life. As the eyes are opened to see how terribly the average Christian life comes short of God's purpose, and how truly the mingled life can be expelled by the power of a new revelation of what God waits to do, the types of Scripture will shine with a new meaning.

A look to the teachings of the New Testament. In Romans, Paul contrasts the life of the Christian under the law with that under grace, the spirit of bondage with the Spirit of adoption. What does this mean but that Christians may still live under the law and its bondage, that they need to come out of this into the full life of grace and liberty through the Holy Spirit, and that, when first they see the difference, nothing is needed but the surrender of faith, to accept and experience what grace will do by the Holy Spirit.

To the Corinthians, Paul writes on some being carnal, and still babes, walking as men after the flesh; others being spiritual, with spiritual discernment and character; to the Galatians, he speaks of the liberty with which Christ, by the Spirit, makes free from the law, in contrast to those who sought to perfect in the flesh, what was begun in the Spirit, and who gloried in the flesh;—all to call them to recognise the danger of the carnal, divided life, and to come at once to the life of faith, the life in the Spirit, which alone is according to God's will.

Everywhere we see in Scripture, what the state of the Church at the present day confesses, that conversion is only the gate that leads into the path of life, that within that gate there is still great danger of mistaking the path, of turning aside, or turning back, and that where this has taken place we are called at once, and with our whole heart, to turn and give ourselves to nothing less than all that Christ is willing to work in us. Just as there are many who have always thought that conversion must be slow, and gradual, and uncertain, because they only take man's powers into account, and cannot understand how it can be sudden and final, so many cannot see how the revelation of the true life of holiness, and the entrance on it by faith out of a life of self-effort and failure, may be immediate and permanent. They look too much to man's efforts, and know not how the second blessing is nothing more nor less than a new vision of what Christ is willing to work in us, and the surrender of faith that yields all to Him.

I would fain hope that what I have written in this book may help some to see that the second blessing is just what they need, is what God by His Spirit will work in them, is nothing but the acceptance of Christ in all His saving power as our strength and life, and is what will bring them into, and fit them for, that full life in the New Covenant, in which God works all in all.

Let me close this note with a quotation from the introduction to a little book just published, *Dying to Self: A Golden Dialogue,* by William Law, with notes by A. M.:

"A great deal has been said against the use of the terms, the Higher Life, the Second Blessing. In Law one finds nothing of such language, but of the deep truth of which they are the, perhaps defective, expression, this book is full. The points on which so much stress is laid in what is called Keswick teaching, stand prominently out in his whole argument. The low state of the average life of believers, the cause of all failure as coming from self-confidence, the need of an entire surrender of the whole being to the operation of God, the call to turn to Christ as the One and Sure Deliverer from the power of self, the Divine certainty of a better life for all who will in self-despair trust Christ for it, and the heavenly joy of a life in which the Spirit of Love fills the heart—these truths are common to both. What makes Law's putting of the truth of special value is the way in which he shows how humility and utter self-despair, with the resignation to God's mighty working in simple faith, is the infallible way to be delivered from self, and have the Spirit of Love fill the heart."

NOTE B—*The Law Written In the Heart*

THE THOUGHT OF THE LAW written in the heart sometimes causes difficulty and discouragement, because believers do not see or feel in themselves anything corresponding to it. An illustration may help to remove the difficulty. There are fluids by which you can write so that nothing is visible, either at once or later, unless the writing be exposed to the sun or the action of some chemical. The writing is there, but one who is ignorant of the process cannot think it is there, and knows not how to make it readable. The faith of a man who is in the secret knows it is there though he see it not.

It is even thus with the new heart. God has put His law into it. "Blessed are the people in whose heart is God's law." But it is there invisibly. He that takes God's promise in faith, knows that it is in his own heart. As long as there is not clear faith on this point, all attempts to find it, or to fulfil that law, will be vain. But when by a simple faith the promise is held fast, the first step is taken to realise it. The soul is then prepared to receive instruction as to what the writing of the law in the heart means. It means, first, that God has implanted in the new heart a love of God's law, and a readiness to do all His will. You may not feel this disposition there, but it is there. God has put it there. Believe this, and be assured that there is in you a Divine nature that says—and you therefore do not hesitate to say it—"I delight to do Thy will, O God!" In the name of God, and in faith, say it.

This writing of the law means, further, that in planting this principle in you, God has taken all that you know of God's will already, and inspired that new heart with the readiness to obey it. It may as yet be written there with invisible writing, and you are not conscious of it. That does not matter. You have here to deal with a Divine and hidden work of the Holy Spirit. Be not afraid to say: Oh, how I love Thy law! God has put the love of it into your heart, the new heart. He has taken away the stony heart; it is by the new heart you have to live.

The next thing implied in this writing of the law, is that you have accepted all God's will, even what you do not yet know, as the delight of your heart. In giving yourself up to God, you gave yourself wholly to His will. That was the one condition of your entering the Covenant; Covenant grace will now provide for teaching you to know, and strengthening you to do, all your Father would have you do.

The whole life in the New Covenant is a life of faith. Faith accepts every promise of the Covenant, is certain that it is being fulfilled, looks confidently to the God of the Covenant to do His work. Faith believes implicitly in the new heart, with the law written in it, because it believes in the promise, and in the God who gave and fulfils the promise.

It may be well to add here that the same truth holds good of all the promises concerning the new heart—they must be accepted and acted on by faith. When we read of "the love of God shed abroad in the heart by the Holy Spirit," of "Christ dwelling in the heart," of "a clean heart," of "loving each other with a clean heart fervently," of "God establishing our heart unblamable in holiness," we must, with the eye of faith, regard these spiritual realities as actually and in very deed existing within us. In His hidden unseen way God is working them there. Not by sight or feeling, but by faith in the Living God and His Word, we know they are as inspiration for the dispositions and inclinations of the new heart. In this faith we are to act, knowing that we have the power to love, to obey, to be holy. The New Covenant gives us a God who works all in us; faith in Him gives us the assurance, above and beyond all feeling, that this God is doing His blessed work.

And if the question be asked what we are to think of all there is within us that contradicts this faith, let us remember what Scripture teaches us of it. We sometimes speak of an old and a new heart. Scripture does not do so. It speaks of the old, the stony, heart, being taken away—the heart, with its will, disposition, affections, being made new with a Divine newness. This new heart is placed in the midst of what Scripture calls the flesh, in which there dwelleth no good thing. We shall find it a great advantage to adhere as closely as possible to Scripture language. It will greatly help our faith even to use the very words God by His Holy Spirit has used to teach us. And it will greatly clear our view for knowing what to think of the sin that remains in us if we think of it and deal with it in the light of God's truth. Every evil desire and affection comes from the flesh, man's sinful natural life. It owes its power greatly to our ignorance of its nature, and our trusting to its help and strength to cast out its evil. I have already pointed out how sinful flesh and religious flesh is one, and how all failure in religion is owing to a secret trust in ourselves. As we accept and make use of what God says of the flesh, we shall see in it the source of all evil in us; we shall say of its temptations: "It is no more I, but sin that dwelleth in me"; we shall maintain our integrity as we maintain a good conscience that condemns us for nothing knowingly done against God's will; and we shall be strong in the faith of the Holy Spirit, who dwells in the new heart, so to strengthen that we need not and "shall not fulfil the lusts of the flesh."

I conclude with an extract of an address by Rev. F. Webster, at Keswick last year, in confirmation of what I have just said:

"Put ye on the Lord Jesus Christ, and make not provision for the flesh, to fulfil the lusts thereof. 'Make no provision for the flesh.' The flesh is there, you know. To deny or ignore the existence of an enemy is to give him a great chance against you; and the flesh is in the believer to the very end, a force of evil to be reckoned with continually, an evil force inside a man, and yet, thank God, a force which can be so dealt with by the power of God, that it shall have no power to defile the heart or deflect the will. The flesh is in you, but your heart may be kept clean moment by moment in spite of the existence of evil in your fallen nature. Every avenue, every opening that leads into the heart, every thought and desire and purpose and imagination of your being, may be closed against the flesh, so that there shall be no opening to come in and defile the heart or deflect the will from the will of God.

"You say that is a very high standard, but it is the Word of God. There is to be no secret sympathy with sin. Although the flesh is there, you are to make it no excuse for sins. You are not to say, I am naturally irritable, anxious, jealous, and I cannot help letting these things crop up; they come from within. Yes, they come from within, but then there need be no provision, no opening in your heart for these things to enter. Your heart can be barricaded with an impassable barrier against these things. 'No provision for the flesh.' Not merely the front door barred and bolted so that you do not invite them to come in, but the side and back door closed too. You may be so Christ-possessed and Christ-enclosed that you shall positively hate everything that is of the flesh.

"'*Make no provision for the flesh.*' The only way to do so is to 'put on the Lord Jesus Christ.' I spoke of the heart being so barricaded that there should be no entrance to it, that the flesh should never be able to defile it or deflect the will from the will of God. How can that be done? By putting on the Lord Jesus Christ. It has been such a blessing to me just to learn that one secret, just to learn the positive side of deliverance—putting on the Lord Jesus Christ."

NOTE C—*George Müller and His Second Conversion*

IN THE LIFE OF GEORGE MÜLLER of Bristol there was an epoch, four years after his conversion, to which he ever after looked back, and of which he often spoke, as his entrance into the true Christian life.

In an address given to ministers and workers after his ninetieth birthday, he spoke thus of it himself:

"That leads to another thought—the full surrender of the heart to God. I *was converted* in November 1825, but I only *came into the full surrender of the heart* four years later, in July 1829. The love of money was gone, the love of place was gone, the love of position was gone, the love of worldly pleasures and engagements was gone. God, God, God alone became my portion. I found my all in Him; I wanted nothing else. And by the grace of God this has remained, and has made me a happy man, an exceedingly happy man, and it led me to care only about the things of God. I ask, affectionately, my beloved brethren, have you fully surrendered the heart to God, or is there this thing or that thing with which you are taken up irrespective of God? I read a little of the Scriptures before, but preferred other books, but since that time the revelation He has made of Himself has become unspeakably blessed to me, and I can say from my heart, God is an infinitely lovely Being. Oh! be not satisfied until in your inmost soul you can say, God is an infinitely lovely Being!"

The account he gives of this change in his journal is as follows. He speaks of one whom he had heard preach at Teignmouth, where he had gone for the sake of his health.

"Though I did not like all he said, yet I saw a gravity and solemnity in him different from the rest. Through the instrumentality of this brother the Lord bestowed a great blessing upon me, for which I shall have cause to thank Him throughout eternity. God then began to show me that the Word of God alone is to be our standard of judgment in spiritual things; that it can only be explained by the Holy Spirit, and that in our day, as well as in former times, He is the Teacher of His people. *The office of the Holy Spirit I had not experimentally understood before that time.* I had not before seen that the Holy Spirit alone can teach us about our state by nature, show us our need of a Saviour, enable us to believe in Christ, explain to us the Scriptures, help us in preaching, etc.

"It was my beginning to understand this point in particular which had a great effect on me; for the Lord enabled me to put it to the test of experience by laying aside commentaries and almost every other book, and simply reading the Word of God and studying it. The result of this was that the first evening that I shut myself into my room to give myself to prayer and meditation over the Scriptures, I learned more in a few hours than I had done during a period of several months previously. *But the particular difference was that I received real strength in my soul in doing so.*

"In addition to this, it pleased the Lord to lead me to see a *higher standard of devotedness* than I had seen before. He led me, in a measure, to see what is my glory in this world, even to be despised, to be poor and mean with Christ. . . . I returned to London much better in body. And as to my soul, *the change was so great that it was like a second conversion.*"

In another passage he speaks thus:

"I fell into the snare into which so many young believers fall, the reading of religious books is preferred to the Scriptures. Now the scriptural way of reasoning would have been: God Himself has condescended to become an author, and I am ignorant of that precious Book which His Holy Spirit has caused to be written; therefore I ought to read again this Book of books most earnestly, most prayerfully, and with much meditation. Instead of acting thus, and being led by my ignorance of the "Word to study it more, my difficulty of understanding it made me careless of reading it, and then, like many believers, I practically preferred for the first four years of my Christian life, the works of uninspired men to the oracles of the Living God. The consequence was that I remained a babe, both in knowledge and grace. In knowledge, I say, for all true knowledge must be derived by the Spirit from the Word. This lack of knowledge most sadly kept me back from walking steadily in the ways of God. For it is the truth makes us free, by delivering us from the slavery of the lusts of the flesh, the lusts of the eyes, and the pride of life. The Word proves it, the experience of the saints proves it, and also my own experience most decidedly proves it. For when it pleased the Lord, in August 1829, to bring me really to the Scriptures, my life and walk became very different.

"If anyone would ask me how he may read the Scriptures most profitably, I would answer him:—

"1. Above all he must seek to have it settled in his own mind *that God alone, by the Holy Spirit, can teach him,* and that, therefore, as God will be inquired for all blessings, it becomes him to seek for God's blessing previous to reading, and also while reading.

"2. He should also have it settled in his mind that though *the Holy Spirit is the best and sufficient Teacher,* yet that He does not always teach immediately when we desire it, and that, therefore, *we may have to entreat Him again and again* for the explanation of certain passages; but that *He will surely teach us* at last, if we will seek for light prayerfully, patiently, and for the glory of God."

Just one more passage, from an address given on his ninetieth birthday·

"For sixty-nine years and ten months he had been a very happy man. That he attributed to two things. He had maintained a good conscience, not wilfully going on in a course he knew to be contrary to the mind of God; he did not, of course, mean that he was perfect; he was poor, weak, and sinful. Secondly, he attributed it to his love of Holy Scripture. Of late years his practice had been four times every year to read through the Scriptures, with application to his own heart, and with meditation; and that day he was a greater lover of God's Word than he was sixty-six years ago. It was this, and maintaining a good conscience, that had given him all these years peace and joy in the Holy Ghost."

In connection with what has been said about the New Covenant being a ministration of the Spirit this narrative is most instructing. It shows us how George Müller's power lay in God's revealing to him the work of the Holy Spirit. He writes that up to the time of that change he had "not experimentally understood the office of the Holy Spirit." We speak much of George Müller's power in prayer; it is of importance to remember that that power was entirely owing to his love of, and faith in, God's Word. But it is of still more importance to notice that his power to believe God's Word so fully was entirely owing to his having learned to know the Holy Spirit as his Teacher. When the words of God are explained to us, and made living within us by the Holy Spirit, they have a power to awaken faith which they otherwise have not. The Word then brings us into contact with God, comes to us as from God direct, and binds our whole life to Him.

When the Holy Spirit thus feeds us on the Word, our whole life comes under His power, and the fruit is seen, not only in the power of prayer, but as much in the power of obedience. Notice how Mr. Müller tells us this, that the two secrets of his great happiness were, his great love for God's Word, and his *ever maintaining a good conscience*, not knowingly doing anything against the will of God. In giving himself to the teaching of the Holy Spirit, as he tells us in his birthday address, he made a full surrender of the entire heart to God, to be ruled by the Word. He gave himself to obey that Word in everything, he believed that the Holy Spirit gave the grace to obey, and so he was able to maintain a walk free from knowingly transgressing God's law. This is a point he always insisted on. So he writes, in regard to a life of dependence upon God: "It will not do—it is not possible—*to live in sin*, and at the same time, by communion with God, to draw down from heaven everything one needs for the life that now is." Again, speaking of the strengthening of faith:

> "It is of the utmost importance that we seek to maintain *an upright heart and a good conscience,* and therefore do not knowingly and habitually indulge in those things which are contrary to the mind of God. All my confidence in God, all my leaning upon Him in the hour of trial, will be gone if I have a guilty conscience, and do not seek to put away this guilty conscience, but still continue to do things which are contrary to His mind."

A careful perusal of this testimony will show us how the chief points usually insisted upon in connection with the second blessing are all found here. There is the full surrender of the heart to be taught and led alone by the Spirit of God. There is the higher standard of holiness which is at once set up. There is the tender desire in nothing to offend God, but to have at all times a good conscience, that testifies that we are pleasing to God. And there is the faith that where the Holy Spirit reveals to us in the Word the will of God, He gives the sufficient strength for the doing of it. "The particular difference," he says of reading with faith of the Holy Spirit's teaching, "was that I received real strength in my soul in doing so."

All centres in this, that we believe in the New Covenant and its promises as a ministration of the Spirit. That belief may come to some suddenly, as to George Müller; or it may dawn upon others by degrees. Let all say to God that they are ready to put their whole heart and life under the rule of the Holy Spirit dwelling in them, teaching them by the Word, and strengthening them by His grace. He enables us to live pleasing to God.

NOTE D—*Canon Battersby*

I DO NOT KNOW THAT I can find a better case by which to illustrate the place Christ, the Mediator of the Covenant, takes in leading into its full blessing than that of the founder of the Keswick Convention, the late Canon Battersby.

It was at the Oxford Convention in 1873 that he witnessed to having "received a new and distinct blessing to which he had been a stranger before." For more than twenty-five years he had been most diligent as a minister of the gospel, and, as appears from his journals, most faithful in seeking to maintain a close walk with God. But he was ever disturbed by the consciousness of being overcome by sin. So far back as 1853 he had written,

> "I feel again how very far I am from enjoying habitually that peace and love and joy which Christ promises. I must confess that I have it not; and that very ungentle and unchristian tempers often strive within me for the mastery."

When in 1873 he read what was being published of the Higher Life, the effect was to render him utterly dissatisfied with himself and his state. There were indeed difficulties he could not quite understand in that teaching, but he felt that he must either reach forward to better things, nothing less than redemption from *all* iniquities, or fall back more and more into worldliness and sin. At Oxford he heard an address on the rest of faith. It opened his eyes to the truth that a believer who really longs for deliverance from sinning must simply take Christ at His word, and reckon, without feeling, on Him to do His work of cleansing and keeping the soul.

> "I thought of the sufficiency of Jesus, and said, I *will rest* in Him, and I did rest in Him. I was afraid lest it should be a passing emotion; but I found that a presence of Jesus was graciously manifested to me in a way I knew not before, and that *I did abide in Him.* I do not want to rest in these emotions, but just to believe, and to cling to Christ as my all."

He was a man of very reserved nature, but felt it a duty ere the close of the Conference to confess publicly his past shortcoming, and testify openly to his having entered upon a new and definite experience.

In a paper written not long after this he pointed out what the steps are leading to this experience. *First,* a clear view of the possibilities of Christian attainment—a life in word and action, habitually governed by the Spirit, in constant communion with God, and continual victory over sin through abiding in Christ. *Then,* the deliberate purpose of the will for a full renunciation of all the idols of the flesh or spirit, and a will-surrender to Christ. And then this last and important step: *We must look up to, and wait upon our ascended Lord for all that we need to enable us to do this.*

A careful perusal of this very brief statement will prove how everything centred here in Christ. The surrender for a life of continual communion and victory is to be to Christ. The strength for that life is to be in Him and from Him, by faith in Him. And *the power* to make the full surrender and rest in Him *was to be waited for from Him alone.*

In June 1875 the first Keswick Convention was held. In the circular calling it, we read:

> "Many are everywhere thirsting that they may be brought to enjoy more of the Divine presence in their daily life, and a fuller manifestation of the Holy Spirit's power, whether in subduing the lusts of the flesh, or in enabling them to offer more effective service to God. It is certainly God's will that His children should be satisfied in regard to these longings, and there are those who can testify that He has satisfied them, and does satisfy them with daily fresh manifestations of His grace and power."

The results of the very first Convention were most blessed, so that after its close he wrote:

> "There is a very remarkable resemblance in the testimonies I have since received as to the nature of the blessing obtained, viz., *the ability given* to make a full surrender to the Lord, and the consequent experience of an abiding peace, far exceeding anything previously experienced."

115

Through all the chief thought, was Christ, first drawing and enabling the soul to rest in Him, and then meeting it with the fulfilment of its desire, the abiding experience of His power to keep it in victory over sin, and communion with God.

And what was the fruit of this new experience? Eight years later Canon Battersby spoke:

"It is now eight years since that I knew this blessing as my own. I cannot say that I have never for a moment ceased to trust the Lord to keep me. But I can say that so long as I have trusted Him, He has kept me; He has been faithful."

ONE WOULD THINK THAT no words could make it plainer than the words of the Covenant state it—that the one difference between Old and New is, that in the latter everything is to be done by God Himself. And yet believers and even teachers do not take it in. And even those who do, find it hard to live it out. Our whole being is so blinded to the true relation to God, His inconceivable Omnipresent Omnipotence working every moment in us is so far beyond the reach of human conception, our little hearts cannot rise to the reality of His Infinite Love making itself one with us, and delighting to dwell in us, and to work all in us that has to be done there—that, when we think we have accepted the truth, we find it is only a thought. We are such strangers to the knowledge of what A GOD really is, as the actual life by which His creatures live. *In Him* we live and move and have our being. And specially is the knowledge of the Triune God too high for us, in that wonderful, most real, and most practical indwelling, to make which possible the Son became Incarnate, and the Holy Spirit was sent forth into our hearts. Only they who confess their ignorance, and wait very humbly and persistently on our Blessed God to teach us by His Holy Spirit what that all-working indwelling is, can hope to have it revealed to them.

It is not long since I had occasion, in preparing a series of Bible Lessons for our Students Association here, to make a study of the Gospel of St. John, and of the life of our Lord as set forth there. I cannot say how deeply I have been afresh impressed with that which I cannot but regard as the deepest secret of His life on earth, *His dependence on the Father.* It has come to me like a new revelation. Some twelve times and more He uses the word *not* and *nothing* of Himself. *Not* My will. *Not* My words. *Not* My honour. *Not* Mine own glory. I can do *nothing* of Myself. I speak *not* of Myself. I came *not* of Myself. I do *nothing* of Myself.

Just think a moment what this means in connection with what He tells us of His life in the Father. "As the Father hath life in Himself, so

He hath given to the Son to have life in Himself" (v. 26). "That all men should honour the Son, even as they honour the Father" (v. 23). And yet this Son, who hath life in Himself even as the Father has, immediately adds (v. 30): "I can of mine own self do *nothing.*" We should have thought that with this life in Himself He would have the power of independent action as the Father has. But no. "The Son can do *nothing* of Himself, but what He seeth the Father do." The chief mark of this Divine life He has in Himself is evidently unceasing dependence, receiving from the Father, by the moment, what He had to speak or do. *Nothing of Myself* is manifestly as true of Him as it ever could be of the weakest or most sinful man. The life of the Father dwelling in Christ, and Christ in the Father, meant that just as truly as when He was begotten of the Father, He received Divine life and glory from Him, so the continuation of that life came only by an eternal process of giving and receiving, as absolute as is the eternal generation itself. The more closely we study this truth and Christ's life in the light of it, the more we are compelled to say, the deepest root of Christ's relationship to the Father, the true reason why He was so well-pleasing, the secret of His glorifying the Father, was this: *Be allowed God to do all in Him.* He only received and wrought out what God wrought in Him. His whole attitude was that of the open ear, the servant spirit, the childlike dependence that waited for all on God.

The infinite importance of this truth in the Christian life is easily felt. The life Christ lived in the Father is the life He imparts to us. We are to abide in Him and He in us, *even as* He in the Father and the Father in Him. And if the secret of His abiding in the Father be this unceasing self-abnegation—"I can do nothing of Myself"—this life of most entire and absolute dependence and waiting upon God, must it not far more be the most marked feature of our Christian life, the first and all-pervading disposition we seek to maintain? In a little book of William Law's, that has just been issued,[10] he specially insists upon this in his so

---

[10] *Dying to Self: A Golden Dialogue.* By William Law. With Notes. The thought is worked out with exceeding power, and the lesson taught that the only thing man

striking repetition of the call, if we would die to self in order to have the birth of Divine love in our souls, to sink down in humility, meekness, patience, and resignation to God. I think that no one who at all enters into this advice, but will feel what new point is given to it by the remembrance of how this entire self-renunciation was not only one of the many virtues in the character of Christ, but, indeed, that first essential one without which God could have wrought nothing in Him, through which God did work all.

Let us make Christ's words our own: *"I can do nothing of Myself."* Take it as the keynote of a single day. Look up and see the Infinite God waiting to do everything as soon as we are ready to give up all to Him, and receive all from Him. Bow down in lowly worship, and wait for the Holy Spirit to work some measure of the mind of Christ in you. Do not be disconcerted if you do not learn the lesson at once: there is the God of love waiting to do everything in him who is willing to be nothing. At moments the teaching appears dangerous, at other times terribly difficult. The Blessed Son of God teaches it us—this was His whole life: I can do nothing of Myself. He is our life; He will work it in us. And when as the Lamb of God He begets this His disposition in us, we shall be prepared for Him to rise on us and shine in us in His heavenly glory.

"Nothing of Myself"—that word spoken eighteen hundred years ago, coming out of the inmost depths of the heart of the Son of God— is a seed in which the power of the eternal life is hidden.

Take it straight from the heart of Christ, and hide it in your heart. Meditate on it till it reveals the beauty of His Divine meekness and humility, and explains how all the power and glory of God could work in Him. Believe in it as containing the very life and disposition which you need, and believe in Christ, whose Spirit dwells in the seed to make it true in you. Begin, in single acts of self-emptying, to offer it to God as the one desire of your heart. Count upon God accepting them, and meeting them with His grace, to make the acts into habits, and the habits into dispositions. And you may depend upon it, there is nothing

---

can do for his salvation is to deny and cease from himself, that God may work in him.

that will lift you so near to God, nothing that will unite you closer to Christ, nothing that will prepare you for the abiding presence and power of God working in you, as the death to self which is found in the simple word—NOTHING OF MYSELF.

This word is one of the keys to the New Covenant Life. As I believe that God is actually to work all in me, I shall see that the one thing that is hindering me is, my doing something of myself. As I am willing to learn from Christ by the Holy Spirit to say truly, *Nothing of myself,* I shall have the true preparation to receive all God has engaged to work, and the power confidently to expect it. I shall learn that the whole secret of the New Covenant is just one thing: GOD WORKS ALL! The seal of the Covenant stands sure: "I the Lord have spoken it, AND I WILL DO IT."

NOTE F—*The Whole Heart*

LET ME GIVE THE PRINCIPAL passages in which the words "the whole heart," "all the heart," are used. A careful study of them will show how whole-hearted love and service is what God has always asked, because He can, in the very nature of things, ask nothing less. The prayerful and believing acceptance of the words will waken the assurance that such wholehearted love and service is exactly the blessing the New Covenant was meant to make possible. That assurance will prepare us for turning to the Omnipotence of God to work in us what may have hitherto appeared beyond our reach.

Hear, first, God's word in Deuteronomy—

4:29: "If thou seek the Lord thy God, thou shalt find Him, if thou *seek Him* with all thy heart and all thy soul."

6:4, 5: "Hear, O Israel, the Lord our God is one Lord ; and thou shalt *love the Lord thy God* with all thy heart, and with all thy soul, and with all thy might."

10:12: "What doth the Lord thy God require of thee but *to fear* the Lord thy God, to *walk in all His ways,* and to *love Him,* and *to serve Him* with all thy heart and all thy soul."

11:13: "Hearken diligently unto My commandments, *to love* the Lord your God, and to *serve Him* with all your heart and all your soul."

13:3: "The Lord your God proveth you, whether ye *love* the Lord your God with all your heart and all your soul."

26:16: "Thou shalt therefore *keep these statutes and do them* with all thy heart and all thy soul."

30:2: "Thou shalt *obey His voice* with all thine heart and with all soul."

30:6: "The Lord thy God will circumcise thine heart, *to love* the Lord thy God with all thine heart and with all thy soul" (see also v. 9, 10).

Take these oft-repeated words as the expression of God's will concerning His people, and concerning yourself; ask if you could wish to give God anything less. Take the last-cited verse as the Divine promise of the New Covenant—that He will circumcise, will so cleanse the heart to love Him with a wholehearted love, that obedience is within your reach; and say whether you will not vow afresh to keep this His first and great commandment.

Listen to Joshua (22:5): "Take diligent heed *to love* the Lord your God, and *to walk* in all His ways, and *to keep* His commandments, and *to cleave* unto Him, and *to serve* Him, with all your heart and with all your soul."

Listen to Samuel (1 Sam. 12:20, 24): "Turn not aside from following the Lord, but *serve the Lord* with all your heart. Only fear the Lord, and *serve Him* in truth with all your heart."

Hear David repeating God's promise to Solomon (1 Kings 2:4): "If thy children take heed to their way, *to walk before Me* in truth with all their heart and all their soul."

Hear God's word concerning David (1 Kings 14:8): "My servant David, *who followed Me* with all his heart, to do that only which was right in Mine eyes."

Hear Solomon in his temple prayer (1 Kings 8:48): "If they *return to Thee* with all their heart and all their soul, hear Thou their prayer."

Listen to what is said of Jehu (2 Kings 10:31): "The Lord said unto Jehu, Thou hast done well in executing that which is right in Mine eyes. *But* Jehu took no heed *to walk* in the law of the Lord with all his heart."

Of Josiah we read (2 Kings 23:3, 25): "The king and all the men of Judah made a covenant with the Lord, *to walk after the Lord,* with all their heart and with all their soul, to perform the words of this covenant that were written in this book. There was no king like him, that *turned to the Lord* with all his heart, and all his soul, and all his might."

The words concerning Asa, in 2 Chron. 15:12, 15, we had as our text.

Of Jehoshaphat, men said (2 Chron. 22:9): "He *sought* the Lord with all his heart."

And of Hezekiah it is written (2 Chron. 31:21): "In every work that he began, to seek his God, he did it with all his heart and prospered."

Oh that all would ask God to give them, by the Holy Spirit, a simple vision of Himself!—claiming, giving, accepting, blessing, delighting in, the love and service of the whole heart—the sacrifice of the whole burnt-offering. Surely they would fall down and join the ranks of those who have given it; and refuse to think of anything as religious life, or worship, or service, but that in which their whole heart went out to God.

Turn to the Psalms. Hear David (9:1; 111:1; 138:1): "I will praise Thee with my whole heart." And in Psalm 119, the Psalm of the way of blessedness: "Blessed who seek Him with the whole heart. With my whole heart have I sought Thee. I shall keep Thy law, yea I shall observe it with my whole heart. I entreated Thy favour with my whole heart. I will keep Thy precepts with my whole heart. I cried with my whole heart." Praise and prayer; seeking God and keeping His precepts; all equally with the whole heart.

Shall we not begin asking more earnestly than ever, as often as we see men engaged in their earthly pursuits in search of money, or pleasure, or fame, or power, with their whole heart, Is this the spirit in which Christians consider that God must be served? Is this the spirit in which I serve Him? *Is not this the one thing needful in our religion?* Lord, reveal unto us Thy will!

Now, just a few words more from the Prophets about the new time, the great change that can come into our lives.

Jer. 24:7: *"I will give them an heart* to know Me that I am the Lord; and they shall be My people and I will be their God; for *they shall return to Me* with their whole heart."

29:13: "Ye shall seek Me, and find Me, when ye shall search for Me with all your heart. *And I will be found of you,* saith the Lord."

32:39-41. Let my reader not be weary of reading carefully these Divine words: they contain the secret, the seed, the living power of a complete transition out of a life in the bondage of halfhearted service, to the glorious liberty of the children of God.—*'I will give them one heart,* that they may fear Me for ever. And I will make an everlasting covenant with them, that *I will not turn away* from them to do them good; but *I will put* My fear in their heart, that they *shall not depart* from Me. Yea, I will rejoice over them to do them good, with *My whole heart and My whole soul!*"

It is to be all God's doing. And He is to do it with His whole heart and His whole soul. It is the vision of this God with His whole heart loving us, longing and delighting to fulfil His promise, and make us wholly His own, that we need. *This vision makes it impossible not to love Him, with our whole heart.* Lord, open our eyes that we may see!

Joel 2:12: "Therefore also now, saith the Lord, *turn ye even* to Me with all your heart."

Zeph. 3:14: "Shout, O Israel ; BE GLAD AND REJOICE WITH ALL THE HEART; the Lord hath taken away thy judgments. HE HATH CAST OUT THINE ENEMY; THE KING OF ISRAEL, THE LORD, IS IN THE MIDST OF THEE; THOU SHALT NOT SEE EVIL ANY MORE."

Now one word from our Lord Jesus (Matt. 22:37): "Jesus said, Thou shalt love the Lord thy God with all thy heart." This is the first and great commandment. This is the sum of that law He came to fulfil for us and in us, *came to enable us to fulfil.* "For what the law could not do, in that it was weak through the flesh, God, sending His own Son, condemned sin in the flesh, that the righteousness of the law might be fulfilled in us who walk after the Spirit."

Praise God! this righteousness of the law—loving God with all the heart, for love is the fulfilling of the law—this righteousness of the law is fulfilled *in* its, who walk after the Spirit. Jesus came to make it possible. He gives His Spirit—the Spirit of life in Christ Jesus—to make it actual. Let us not fear to give ourselves a whole burnt-offering, acceptable to God; loving Him with all our heart and mind and strength.

May I ask the reader just once again to peruse Chapter 6, on "The Everlasting Covenant," and Chapter 18, on "Entering the Covenant: With All the Heart." And say then, if you have never yet entered fully into this covenant of the whole heart, whether you are not ready to do it now. God demands, God works, God is, oh, so infinitely worthy, of the whole heart! Fear not to say He shall have it. You may confidently count upon the blessed Lord Jesus, the Surety of the Covenant, whose it is to make it true in you by His Spirit, to enable you to exercise the faith that knows that God's power will work what He has promised. In His Name say:

With my whole heart I do love Thee!

90489742R00071

Made in the USA
Middletown, DE
23 September 2018